Images

of the

Young Child

Collected Essays on Development and Education

David Elkind

A 1992–93 NAEYC Comprehensive Membership benefit

National Association for the Education of Young Children—Washington, DC

To the memory of Ray Williams, dear friend, respected colleague, and outstanding mentor to early childhood educators.

About the Author

David Elkind is Professor of Child Study at Tufts University in Medford, Massachusetts, and was formerly Professor of Psychology, Psychiatry, and Education at the University of Rochester. He did his doctoral studies at the University of California, Los Angeles, and in 1964–65 he was a National Science Foundation Senior Postdoctoral Fellow at Piaget's Institut d'Epistemologie Genetique in Geneva. A prolific writer of research, theoretical, and popular articles and books, Elkind is perhaps best known for three very influential books—*All Grown Up and No Place to Go, The Hurried Child,* and *Miseducation: Preschoolers at Risk.* David Elkind served as president of the National Association for the Education of Young Children from 1986 to 1988.

Photo credits: Cover 1–© Michaelyn Straub; p. 1–© Emily Maratta; p. 5–© The Franklin School; p. 8–© BmPorter/Don Franklin; p. 13–© Marietta Lynch; p. 17–© Toni H. Liebman; p. 21–© Marilyn Nolt; p. 25–© Rich Rosenkoetter; p. 31–© Marietta Lynch; p. 35–© Cleo Freelance Photo; p. 41–© F. Wardle; p. 45–© Marietta Lynch; p. 46–© Renaud Thomas; p. 49– © Florence Sharp; p. 52–© Judy Burr; p. 55–© Marietta Lynch; p. 58–© Elisabeth Nichols; p. 63–© Elisabeth Nichols; p. 67–© Cleo Freelance Photo; p. 71–© Marietta Lynch; p. 74–© Kate Sharp; p. 77–© Anne Crabbe; p. 80–© F. Wardle; p. 85–© Jim West; p. 88–© Private Eye Photography; p. 93–© F. Wardle

National Association for the Education of Young Children
1509 16th Street, N.W.
Washington, DC 20036–1426
202–232–8777 or 1–800–424–2460

The National Association for the Education of Young Children (NAEYC) attempts through its publications program to provide a forum for discussion of major issues and ideas in our field. We hope to provoke thought and promote professional growth. The views expressed or implied are not necessarily those of the Association. NAEYC wishes to thank the author, who donated much time and effort to develop this book as a contribution to our profession.

Library of Congress Catalog Card Number: 93–086828
ISBN Catalog Number: 0–935989–58–7
NAEYC #343

Editor: Carol Copple; *Copyeditor:* Betty Nylund Barr; *Design and production:* Jack Zibulsky and Penny Atkins; *Editorial assistance:* Julie Andrews, Valarie Banks, Millie Riley, and Roma White

Printed in the United States of America

Contents

Foreword

This collection is only the latest of David Elkind's many contributions to early childhood education and, indeed, to the well-being of children in America. Beginning in the early 1960s, Elkind played a prominent role in replicating and extending the work of Jean Piaget and bringing it to the attention of American educators. Since the '70s he has been a vocal critic of the trend to make education of young children more formal and academic.

Three of David Elkind's most widely read books—*All Grown Up and No Place To Go* (1981), *The Hurried Child* (1984), and *Miseducation: Preschoolers at Risk* (1987)—have reached many readers beyond the early childhood field with his strongly felt message: that we are expecting children to grow up too fast, too soon, and educating them in ways that do not suit their developmental stage. This message Elkind advocated eloquently during his tenure as NAEYC's president from 1986 to 1988. Extremely effective in communicating with those outside the early childhood field, David Elkind has succeeded in spurring a great many people—including those in the traditional education establishment and the media—to rethink old assumptions about children, education, and contemporary society.

As we read through the large body of David Elkind's writings in selecting the essays for this collection, we were struck with his longstanding interest in the societal context of childhood, that is, how we perceive children and how our perceptions, in turn, shape our approaches to education and child rearing. This common thread in Elkind's work is reflected in the title of this volume, *Images of the Young Child*. Each essay in the collection reminds us that our educational and child care practices flow directly from our images of the young child— a crucial reminder as we strive to make early childhood education developmentally appropriate: we will not get far until there is a virtual sea change in perceptions of the young child in our society as a whole.

In NAEYC's ongoing efforts to help bring about such a fundamental change, we are grateful to David Elkind for allowing us to publish this collection. In each of the essays, he compellingly illuminates the developmental image of the child and how this image should shape our educational practice.

–Carol Copple, Editor

–Marilyn Smith, Executive Director

Preface

My introduction to early childhood education was accidental rather than deliberate. I was trained as an adult clinical psychologist and took a postdoctoral fellowship at the Austen Riggs Center in Stockbridge, Massachusetts, to study with David Rappaport, a renowned Freudian scholar. Before I arrived at the center, I began receiving from Rappaport books that were not by Freud but rather by a psychologist I had never heard of in any of my undergraduate or graduate courses in psychology. With considerable disappointment and much reluctance, I began to read the books of Jean Piaget.

I had been trained in the logical positivist scientific tradition, which insists that to be valid, all concepts must be operationally defined; that is, defined in terms of how they are to be measured. Equally important, this scientific tradition insists that all experiments be strictly controlled and that virtually every variable be quantified. As I began to read Piaget's books, I was incredulous because there were no operationally defined concepts (I once started counting the number of different definitions of assimilation that Piaget gave in *The Origins of Intelligence* and gave up after reaching 150), no controls, and little if any quantification. I decided to replicate Piaget's work in a strictly scientific manner to demonstrate that his findings could not be verified when "proper" experimental methodology was employed.

Rappaport had me read *The Child's Conception of Number,* and we discussed it at length. It seemed a good starting point to demonstrate the weakness of the Piagetian findings. Austen Riggs had a small nursery school where some of the patients could help care for the children. I asked for permission to test some of the children and, armed with my box of pennies and clay balls, visited the nursery school. The teacher suggested that I spend several days observing so that the children would be more comfortable with me once I began to interview them. This was my accidental introduction to early childhood education. Fortunately, this nursery school had an excellent early childhood program, so my first experience set a standard for me by which to gauge the many other classrooms that I would later encounter.

When I started interviewing children, I was amazed to discover that they responded much as Piaget said they would. In addition, my quantitative methods made it clear that the age differences Piaget observed were indeed statistically significant. At that point I underwent something of a scientific conversion experience. From being a harsh critic of Piaget, I became a staunch advocate. Moreover, I discovered that I enjoyed working with children and that I wanted to be a child psychologist rather than a clinician working with adults. After my stint at Austen Riggs, I went for two years of additional clinical training with children at the Beth Israel Hospital in Boston.

I kept up with my Piagetian experiments. Because I had no grant money, I did all of the interviewing myself. That meant that for the next 10 years or so, I spent a great deal of time in nursery and elementary schools. I worked in Montessori schools to determine if perhaps the Montessori methods might accelerate cognitive and perceptual growth. As a result of some of my publications, John Goodlad asked me to visit nursery schools around the country that serve low-income children. A friend who directed a speech and hearing clinic got me interested in American Indian children, and I did a number of studies at reservations with Apache and Oglala Sioux children. When I went to study with Piaget in Geneva, I interviewed children from Switzerland, other parts of Europe, and the Middle East.

I recite this personal history only to demonstrate that my interest in early childhood education is of long standing and is built upon many, many years spent in early childhood settings and working with children and teachers from many different ethnic, racial, and cultural backgrounds. The essays in this book thus derive from my hands-on experience with young children, living and working in early childhood settings, not just from research and scholarly works. Although my introduction to young children was accidental and although I enjoy working with young people at all of the developmental stages, you may sense in these pages that early childhood is by far my favorite age period.

The essays in this book were written at different times and for different audiences. Reading them over, however, I recognize that I always tried to combine broad concepts with concrete examples and suggestions for practice. At times I have also introduced concepts of my own where I believed that there were none to cover the particular phenomena I wanted to describe. Indeed, if these articles have any special claim, it is that they attempt to use practice to generate theory as much as they try to translate theory into practice.

I hope that this collection of writings conveys some of the great fun that I have had—and the enormous respect that I have acquired—working with young children and their teachers over these many years.

—David Elkind
November 1993

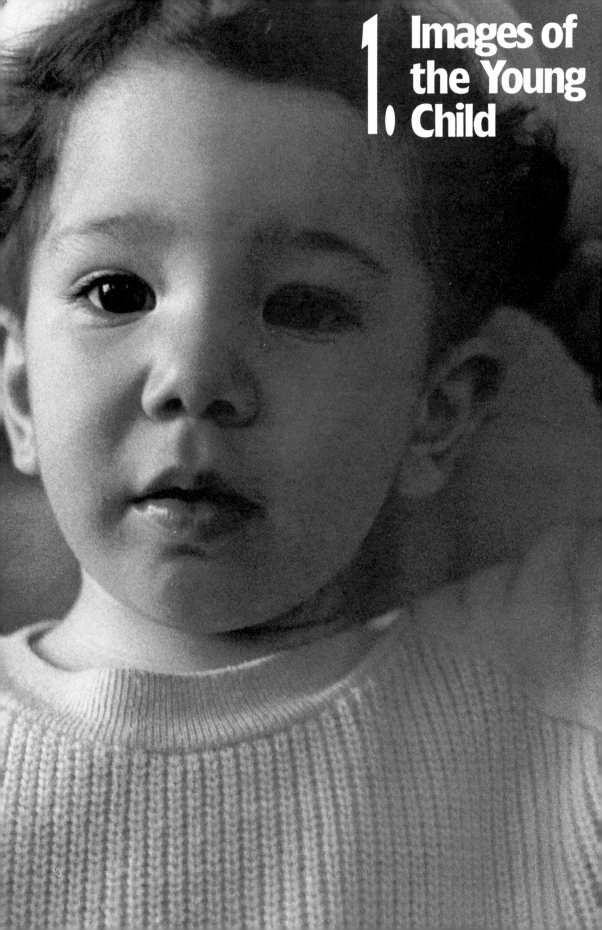

1. Images of the Young Child

*A*s a young investigator–like most young researchers, I suppose–
I tended to idealize science. I believed that scientific knowledge
was objective and unprejudiced. I also assumed that our scientific
knowledge determined how we viewed the world and interacted
with it. With maturity came the growing realization that science
is not always objective nor studiously even-handed and that
scientific knowledge is determined by the social dynamics of
history and colored by the personalities of the investigators who
explore different domains.

One way of looking at the essays in this section is as a kind of
route map of my progressive exploration of the many social-
historical and personality dynamics that determine how we view,
rear, and educate children at any given time and place in history.
The first essay, "The Child Yesterday, Today, and Tomorrow,"
looks at how children have been regarded over recorded history.
The second essay, "Piaget and Montessori in the Classroom,"
examines the different ways in which two of the most renowned
figures in early childhood education view the development and
education of young children. The third essay, "Work Is Hardly
Child's Play," looks not so much at children but rather at
children's play and how it has been conceptualized by different
investigators. In the last essay in this section, "Development in
Early Childhood," I took a somewhat different tack and sought
to summarize our contemporary scientific knowledge about child
growth and development. This essay is included here not merely as a
kind of capstone to the other discussions but also because it introduces
still another way of looking at the development of young children that
I believe is important both theoretically and practically.

Another discovery that comes with maturity as an investigator
is that wrong ideas are likely to catch on more quickly than right
ones. Although many of my colleagues would probably protest, I
believe that socialization does not come about as a consequence
of the child's growing ability to take the other person's point of
view; this, in fact, is difficult to do at all stages of development.
Rather, I believe that children are socialized by learning **frames**–
the implicit rules, expectancies, and understandings that govern
repeated social situations. A brief discussion of frames appears
toward the end of "Development in Early Childhood."

The theme of this section, then, is difference–the many different ways that we can look at young children and the activities that they engage in. Appreciation of difference is important; it keeps us humble and aware that ours is not the only perspective. On the other hand, if one believes that there are no generalities–no overriding, transcendental truths–this can lead to a kind of "soft relativism" such that one does not take a stand on anything. There is a middle ground, and that is **consensus.** *I am often amused to see that early childhood educators who are at opposite theoretical extremes behave quite similarly when they are with children. Teachers and caregivers who work effectively and successfully with children share a common experiential base that should be the starting point for reaching a consensus on best ways to rear and educate young children.*

The Child Yesterday, Today, and Tomorrow

The child is a gift of nature; the image of the child is man's creation. The image of the child, rather than nature's gift, determines educational practice in any historical epoch. And the image of the child, man's creation, is as often wrong as it is correct. False images are more powerful and more easily grasped than are true ones. In the present, as in the past, our task as educators of young children is not simply to be true to nature's gift but also to fight against the false images that, in any era, threaten the healthy education of young children.

Past images

The image of the child in antiquity was that of a young citizen who had to be educated in the laws and culture of society. Boys and girls in Babylon went to school at age six, and even poor children learned to read and write, although their books were bricks and their writing tools a reed and damp clay. In ancient Greece boys went to school at age seven. In ancient Rome women had a more equal place than they did in other ancient societies—both boys and girls went to school, where discipline was strict and they learned to write with a stylus and wax tablet.

During the Middle Ages children fared less well, and the prevailing image of the child was that of chattel, or a piece of property, consistent with the ideology of serfdom. The medieval castle was no place for a child, built as it was for defense rather than for comfort. The children of serfs worked and lived with the animals. Discipline was strict and punishment harsh. In England children enjoyed a brief, golden era during the reign of Good Queen Bess. And during this era, the faithful nanny begins to appear in folklore and literature. Toward the end of the 17th century, the struggle between Cavaliers and Puritans was reflected in their dissimilar images of children. The Cavaliers held a mixed image of the child as part nuisance, part plaything. In contrast, the Puritans saw the child as tainted with original sin. "Your child," wrote James Janeway, "is never too young to go to hell."

In the United States our images of children changed with our rapidly changing society. In colonial times children were seen as financial assets who could help work the farm or be apprenticed outside the home at an early age; children of slaves were an extreme example of this image, but they were not the only children who labored from dawn to dark. With the industrial revolution, children, especially the sons and daughters of immigrants and the poor, came to be seen as cheap factory workers until the cruelty of child labor was made public. The ensuing social-reform movement transformed the image of the child from one of cheap factory labor to one of apprentice to factory work. Instead of being sent to the factory, children were sent to school to prepare them to work in factories. Just as factory whistles signaled the beginning and the end of the work day, school bells signaled the beginning and the end of the school day. Children, like their parents, carried lunch pails to be opened at the noon bell.

As we see, societies have held many different images of children, some of which were more beneficial than others to children's health, welfare, and education. And, at any given point in history, some people have been critical of the image of the child that was current at that time. Often this criticism took the form of an attack on parents and parenting, but in fact it was an attack upon the then-"accepted" image of the child. A review of these past attacks is instructive. It tells us that the image of the child at any point in history does not go unchallenged

and that the challengers at any time often come from the ranks of early childhood educators.

The criticism of prevailing images of the child has a long history. For his ideal Republic, Plato wanted children to be raised by professional child caretakers, and St. Augustine proclaimed, "Give me other mothers and I will give you other worlds." Rousseau's opening statement in *Emile* (1955), which states that everything is good as it comes from the hands of the Maker and deteriorates in the hands of man, is an indictment of the image of the child as a young savage who had to be socialized.

Pestalozzi and Froebel did not criticize parents directly but did believe that parents needed to be given a truer image of the child and that this would result in more healthy childrearing practices. Parent education was an important component of early childhood education practiced by Pestalozzi and Froebel. Pestalozzi's book *How Gertrude Teaches Her Children* (1898), which is subtitled *An Attempt To Help Mothers Teach Their Own Children*, reflects this emphasis on training parents. The same theme was repeated in Froebel (1893).

Maria Montessori never criticized parents either, but she had less faith in parent education than did her predecessors. Like Plato she wanted children reared by professionals, not by parents. To her, childrearing was too important a task to be left to untrained parents, whose image of the child gave too little credit to their budding intellectual powers.

In the past, the prevailing image of the child that dictated childrearing and education was determined by a complex set of social, economic, and cultural factors that may have had little or nothing to do with the natural child. And since early times, critics have challenged the prevailing concept of the child. These critics fought to replace the false image of the child with a more realistic one that would provide for a healthier, happier, and more productive child life.

20th-century images

Historically, predominant images of the child were derived from the prevailing political, social, or religious ethos. What is remarkable about modern images of the child is that they are, or are said to be, scientific in origin. Unfortunately their scientific origin has not rendered them any more valid than those images having social, political, or religious derivations. In some ways the scientific origin of some of the contemporary images of the child makes them even more difficult to combat than previous images. I now want to usurp the role of critic and review and comment upon three modern images of the child that have contributed to what I call miseducation, that is, putting children at risk for no purpose.

The sensual child

The advent of Freudian psychology gave rise to the image of the sensual child. In this view, the child was "polymorphous perverse" in the sense of having the whole gamut of sexual instincts and proclivities that were once reserved to adults (Freud, 1905). In Freudian terms, children whose sexual instincts were unduly repressed were destined to become neurotic. The childrearing and educational implications of this image of the sensual child were straightforward: children had to be allowed to express themselves, and play was the natural medium of self-expression. With adequate self-expression at home and at school, children would develop healthy personalities and their intelligence would take care of itself.

Like so many images of the child, this idea contains a partial truth. Freud made clear that a certain amount of repression was healthy, indeed necessary, for people to live in a society. It was not repression but *excessive* repression that produced neuroses, but that point was sometimes lost on those who fought for expression at all costs.

The malleable child

Another image of the child that has dominated contemporary thought has come from the anthropologists who were concerned with the conflict between generations. The leading writers of this genre were Kingsley Davis, Ruth Benedict, and Margaret Mead. Although they differed in detail, they were all making the same point: children are plastic and adaptable in contrast to adults, who are rigid and unadaptable. Children, these writers argued, are better suited to social change than are adults.

Davis (1940), for example, argued that adults are locked into the orientation they received as children and this makes appreciating the changed circumstances of their offspring difficult, if not impossible, hence the generational conflict. Benedict (1938) said that adults are independent and children are dependent, and that the adult's inability to deal with the child's growing independence was the cause of the generational conflict. Margaret Mead (1970) argued that in a rapidly changing culture, children, who are free of ingrained habits of thought, are better able to adapt to new and changing technologies than are adults.

This image of child malleability in contrast to adult rigidity is sometimes misinterpreted. Anthropologists are referring to change in society, *not* change within the immediate family. When a family moves, children have more trouble with the change than do adults; and while divorce may be hard on adults, it is certainly much harder on children. Children thrive on consistency, stability, and security, while adults seek new experience and adventure. Children adapt less easily to change within the family than do adults, but the reverse image—fostered by misapplication of social scientists' ideas about change in society—persists and contributes to miseducation.

The introduction of computers into early childhood education and the teaching of programming to young children is a direct offshoot of this malleability concept. It harks back to the concept of "formal discipline," according to which learning a particular subject sharpens the mental faculties. Young people learned Latin and Greek because this was thought to improve their language facility, and they learned geometry to enhance their reasoning powers. Children, no less than adults, can work with computers without knowing programming. Knowing programming is nice, but it is neither a necessary nor a sufficient condition for learning to use a computer. Moreover, because programming is difficult, insisting that young children learn it runs the risk of smothering their interest in using this technology.

Computers are now part of our environment, and it makes sense to have them in early childhood classrooms. The real problem is finding good, developmentally appropriate software for children. A few such programs (like Delta Drawing) are now available.

Some children have a natural affinity for computers and may spend a great deal of time with them. Other children do not have such an affinity, and they should have the choice of using the computer or not. What we have to avoid is the misguided idea that we need to teach young children programming before they can use computers successfully. The majority of adults who use computers, like me, know nothing of progamming and probably never will. The risk is that children will get turned off before they have a chance to see what else computers can do. A heavy emphasis on programming is a good example of miseducation, of putting children at risk for no purpose.

In the same way, I am often asked about programs to inform young children about the threats of nuclear war. Presumably, children have to be exposed to this idea at an early age so they will be better prepared for a nuclear holocaust if or when it comes. Even if we accept this shaky premise, we must recognize that the concept of nuclear war is completely foreign to young children, who do not even have a conception of biological death, much less of millions of people and the power of nuclear weapons to destroy them. Recent suggestions that young children be taught about AIDS also stem from this wrongheaded image of child malleability.

To be sure, children are fresh learners to the extent that they are not handicapped by previous ideas and concepts, but this does not mean that they are ready to learn everything and anything—far from it. Their openness to learning is limited, and we must recognize these limitations. There is a time and a place for everything, and early childhood education is not the time nor the place to teach children computer programming, the threat of nuclear war, or, for that matter, the dangers of AIDS.

The competent infant

Perhaps the most pervasive and pernicious contemporary image of the child is one that has been promoted by psychologists writing in the 1960s. Responding to the civil rights movement, to the War on Poverty, and to the inadequacies of the educational system, many writers gave voice to a vision of childhood that would undo these wrongs—and undo them at an early age. All of these wrongs, they said, could be righted if we only got to children early enough. The result was a new image of infants and young children as having much more capacity to learn academic skills than children—regardless of background—actually have. Although all young children have intellectual abilities and their thinking should be encouraged, their psychological stage of development must always be considered.

In his book *The Process of Education,* Jerome Bruner (1962) voiced his now-famous hypothesis that you can "teach any child any subject matter at any age in an intellectually responsible way." Bruner was really speaking to curriculum writers and probably did not fully appreciate the extent to which his hypothesis would be accepted by the public not as a hypothesis but as a fact. It has also

become the motto of entrepreneurs hawking flashcards to parents with the proclamation that you can teach a young child "anything."

But is it true? It is only true if you either redefine the child or redefine the subject matter. The curriculum writers of the 1960s, academicians such as Max Beberman at the University of Illinois or Robert Karplus at Berkeley, knew their subject matter but not young children. The curricula they designed in effect redefined the competence of children without recourse to children's actual abilities and limitations. Variable base arithmetic, for example, was said to be easier for children to learn than base-ten arithmetic, but even parents had trouble with variable base arithmetic! Academicians also claimed that children would learn math better if it were introduced as a language. Instead of answering "What is the sum of $2 + 2$?" children were asked to "Make this sentence true."

The error here came from confusing what is simple to an expert in a subject with what is simple for the novice. Simplicity is the end result of learning a skill or a discipline, not its starting point. Reading is simple once you know how, but it is far from simple when you first start out. Understanding multiple base arithmetic may be simple once you know base ten but not if you don't. Understanding the relation of language to mathematics is simple if you have a firm grasp of language and mathematics but not if you don't. We have to always be aware of the danger of assuming that the end point for us as adults should be the starting point for children.

The other side of Bruner's hypothesis required redefining the subject matter. When an infant who responds to flashcards is said to be "reading" or doing "math," these subject matters have been drastically redefined. Suppose, for example, that I tell you that I can balance 100 pounds on my finger; you would not believe me. But suppose I take out a 3 × 5" card and write "100 pounds" on it. Now I put the card on my finger, and voilà, I am holding 100 pounds on my finger. Claiming to teach infants to read and do math is the same; it is a sleight-of-hand trick accomplished by redefining what is usually meant by reading and by math.

People are taken in by this trickery and really believe that they are teaching their children these subjects, and this trickery has another negative fallout effect: Redefining the subject matter makes it much easier to acquire. Parents then believe that their child who is "reading" flashcards at age two is a budding genius, but they will ultimately be disappointed. Unfortunately, making a task easier does not make children brighter.

Another contribution to the image of the competent infant came from educational psychologist Benjamin Bloom (1964) who argued from statistical summaries of IQ data that four-year-olds had attained half of their intellectual ability and that it was incumbent upon us to impose formal learning on young children because otherwise we might lose out on this period of phenomenal mental growth. This idea that you must teach as much as possible to young children because their minds are growing so rapidly has become part of the contemporary folk wisdom and is deeply ingrained in our contemporary image of the child.

But is it true? Bloom was talking about mental test data, not about mental growth. Because infants and young children are not good test takers, their intelligence test performance is not a good index of their later test performance. By age 4, however, the child is sufficiently verbal and has sufficient ability to concentrate attention, and her or his test performance is a better index of true ability. From the test score a child attains at age 4, you can predict with about 50% accuracy what that child's test score will be at age 17, and that is all that a child attaining half of her or his mental ability at age 4 means. It does not mean that at age 4 the child has half of all the knowledge, skills, and values she or he will ever have. It does not mean that if a child attains an IQ of 100 at age 4, she or he will attain an IQ score of 200 at age 17. It does not mean that a child at age 4 is a better learner than she or he will be at age 17. Even granting that mental growth is rapid during

the early years of life, we would not necessarily conclude that children would benefit from formal, teacher-directed learning in these years. During periods of rapid mental growth, children seek out the stimuli to nourish themselves mentally. We serve them best by providing an environment rich in materials to observe, explore, manipulate, and talk, write, and think about. You do not prune during the growing season.

A third writer who has contributed to the contemporary image of competent infants is J. McV. Hunt. In his book *Intelligence and Experience* (1961), Hunt surveyed a great deal of evidence and concluded that intelligence was malleable; he contended that his contemporaries mistakenly saw it as fixed and immutable. However, no reputable psychologist ever claimed that intelligence was fixed. For instance, Florence Goodenough (1954) pointed out that there is evidence that environmental factors account for between 20% and 40% of an individual's IQ.

Until the 1960s, however, psychologists were mainly concerned with middle-class children who presumably had maximized their environmental potential. Only when attention turned to low-income children who had less than optimal environmental input did the significance of environmental input become a matter of concern. Consider the following analogy. Suppose you place a group of undernourished children on a full calorie, well-balanced diet. Surely such children will make significant gains in both height and weight, but children who are already on a full-calorie, well-balanced diet will not make similar gains. The potential benefits of an improved program are relative to the quality of the previous environment.

The idea of intellectual malleability has become common currency among parents who are told that with the proper program of stimulation they can have a "brighter child" or they can raise their child's IQ. No evidence exists that children growing up in an environment where they are talked to, played with, and read to, and that is rich in things to look at, listen to, and explore will derive additional benefit from prescribed exercises and symbolic materials. If anything, most middle-class children today are over- rather than understimulated.

The last contributor to the image of the competent child is not a psychologist but a historian. In his book *Centuries of Childhood* (1962), Phillip Aries argues that childhood is a social invention and that no such concept existed in the Middle Ages, when children were depicted and treated much as adults. The implication is that for the last couple of hundred years we have been coddling children and infantalizing them and ignoring their true competence and abilities. This thesis fit in neatly with the other ideas about infant competence and gave it a historical dimension.

More recent historians of childhood, like Pollack (1983), have shown that Aries was wrong. Even in those eras that Aries describes as lacking a concept of childhood, diaries of parents clearly show that adults appreciated that children were different from themselves and had to be treated differently. Sir Francis Bacon, writing in the 16th century, even talked about the value of "allowances" and the negative effects of not giving a child a sufficient allowance. He suggested that "The proof is best when men keep their authority towards their children, but not their purse."

These four ideas, then—that a child can be taught any subject at any age; that children have half their intellectual ability at age four (due to the rapid mental growth in the early years of life); that the IQ is malleable; and that childhood is an invention—all emerged in the 1960s to form a new image of child competence. To be sure, researchers in the '60s and '70s, largely through advances in technology, were able to discern that infants have greater perceptual, cognitive, and linguistic capacities than had been formerly detected. It was found, for example, that even the fetus can discriminate the mother's voice from other voices. The investigators publishing such research did not intend it to be used as a justification for earlier instruction. Indeed, when one researcher found that his work had been used as a rationale for a "prenatal university," he published an article on "the hurried fetus."

Thus, although the image of the competent child counteracted a previous image that underestimated child competence, the new image went to the other extreme. Ideas meant to improve the conditions of low-income children have been taken over by middle-class parents and have become the rationale for much of the miseducation of young children today.

As in the past, we not only have to assert the values of child-centered early childhood education but we must also struggle to reveal the concepts of early childhood malleability and competence for what they are, namely, distortions of how young children really grow and learn.

Future images

Given the brief history I have just outlined, we may reasonably predict that the false images of children today will be replaced by equally false images tomorrow. I have no crystal ball, only a belief that history is prologue and that the image of the child at any point in history always fills the predominant parent needs and defenses of that developmental epoch. We have to ask, then, what the needs of future parents will be and how these will be reflected in a new image of the child.

Our society is already a service and information society, with more than 70% of our population in these occupations. I believe that we will eventually get high-quality child care for all youngsters who need it and that people who care for infants and young children will have positions of respect and will be paid well. We may even have parent professionals to care for and rear other people's children. This will not happen immediately and without a great deal of hard work and pain, but I do believe that we will get there.

What then? What new image will emerge when the image of the malleable, competent child has run its course? What sort of image of the child will be most in keeping with the needs of tomorrow's parents? If present trends continue, parents will probably spend less time than ever parenting. Once parents no longer feel guilty or uncomfortable about this, the need for the image of child intellectual competence will diminish. In its place will emerge a new image of child social sophistication and self-sufficiency. In an information and service society, these are requisite skills. We already see hints of this in the current emphasis on social cognition. Psychologists are eager to point out that Piaget was wrong and that infants and young children are much more socially skilled than we gave them credit for being.

Although children may be more socially proficient and self-sufficient than we may have recognized, they will not be as socially proficient as the image of social sophistication will have us believe. The cycle will once again repeat itself: The next generation of early childhood educators will challenge the new image of the child as, to use the computer term that may well become the catchword of this new image, *an expert system* with respect to social interaction. The next generation will once again reassert the values of sound early childhood education.

Our task as early childhood educators, then, is unending. Each generation presents a new challenge and a new battle, and it is a battle that we can never really win because each new generation is prone to the same mistakes; yet if we do not fight, it is a battle we can most assuredly lose. For those of us in early childhood education, the battle is well worth fighting, and even if we fall before our time, we can take comfort in the knowledge that there will always be others, sufficiently committed to the well-being of young children, to carry on the fight.

References

Aries, P. (1962). *Centuries of childhood.* New York: Knopf.

Benedict, R. (1938). Continuities and discontinuities in cultural conditioning. *Psychiatry, 1,* 161–167.

Bloom, B. (1964). *Stability and change in human behavior.* New York: Wiley.

Bruner, J. (1962). *The process of education.* Cambridge, MA: Harvard University Press.

Davis, K. (1940). The sociology of parent–youth conflict. *American Sociological Review, 5,* 523–525.

Freud, S. (1905). *Three essays on sexuality.* New York: Basic.

Froebel, F. (1893). *The education of man.* New York: Appleton.

Goodenough, F. (1954). The measurement of mental health in children. In L. Carmichael (Ed.), *Manual of child psychology* (pp. 75–76). New York: Knopf.

Hunt, J. McV. (1961). *Intelligence and experience.* New York: Ronald.

Mead, M. (1970). *Culture and commitment.* New York: Natural History Press/Doubleday.

Pestalozzi, J.H. (1898). *How Gertrude teaches her children.* Syracuse, NY: C.W. Badeen.

Pollack, L. (1983). *Forgotten children.* Cambridge: Cambridge University Press.

Rousseau, J.J. (1955). *Emile* (B. Foxley, Trans.). New York: Dutton.

The original version of this essay appeared in *Young Children,* (1987), 42(4), 6–11.

Piaget and Montessori in the Classroom

Classroom practice, of whatever variety, presupposes a particular conception of the child. This essay describes four components of Piaget's and Montessori's conceptions of the child, together with examples of the sort of educational practice that follows from them.

Recently I had the opportunity to visit and observe in two different Montessori classrooms. One was not at all like the other. In one room several boys were making a train with the blocks usually used for the pink tower (the pink, size-graded blocks are usually used to build a tower, with the largest block on the bottom and successively smaller ones on top; the "pink tower" is used to teach size relationships). The teacher observed this but did not intervene because the boys were clearly involved in what they were do-

ing. Something similar occurred in the other classroom, but the teacher in this room did get involved. She showed the boys how to build a tower with the blocks and said that unless they were prepared to build a tower, they should not take out the blocks.

I begin with this example because it illustrates the close connection between our conceptions of the child and of learning, and classroom practice. From a theoretical point of view, one could find ample justification for either teacher behavior. If one assumes that a child can learn from his or her own self-directed activity, then allowing children to manipulate materials in their own way makes sense. On the other hand, if one assumes that certain ways of using the materials are far more beneficial than others, then discouraging children from any other uses of the materials makes sense. In short, every classroom practice presupposes a particular conception about children and about how children learn. Any discussion of classroom applications of Piaget must then be presented in the context of his conceptions of the child and of learning. In this essay I present four aspects of Piaget's conception of the child and relate these to aspects of Montessori's theory and practice.

The child as capable of self-regulation

Piaget, like Montessori, believes that children have the potential for self-regulated activity, for using materials in such a way as to nourish their intellectual growth. Usually such activity has direction, organization, and self-correction in relation to the materials, but we must realize that self-regulational activity is a *potential* form of activity, not necessarily a spontaneous one. Whether or not a child can engage in self-regulated activity will depend upon her or his past history and upon the environmental circumstances. This correlation is analogous to the "norm of reaction" of biology. Some species of insects, for example, have the genetic potential for eye color from red to black. Which eye color they ultimately have depends upon the environment in which the insect develops. Something similar occurs in human beings. A child with a potential for asthma, for example, may show no symptoms if he or she is born and grows up in Arizona. Symptoms may appear, however, if that person moves to the east coast.

In the same way the child has a range of potential behaviors, only some of which are self-regulational. Children can, for example, engage in behavior that is self-destructive or other-destructive. A child who builds pink towers long after having acquired the basic concepts may be engaging in defensive avoidance actions. A child who uses the blocks as missiles to hurl at his neighbors is also not

engaging in self-regulational behavior. In short, for Piaget, as for Montessori, self-regulational activity is but one of many possible activities children can engage in.

To my mind, Montessori's genius was best shown in her understanding that certain environments—prepared environments— were necessary to release and encourage self-regulational behavior. The materials she discovered and invented for encouraging self-regulated behavior are excellent models for all educational materials, but the environment itself may not be sufficient to encourage self-regulational behavior in all children. Some children come to us from environments that either have discouraged self-regulation or permitted children too much freedom. Such children may not be able to profit from the new environment as long as they expect it to be like the one from which they came.

We come back now to my initial example of the two teachers, in which I assumed that the children in both classrooms were capable of self-regulation in that setting and that teacher response was therefore a function of their differential conceptions of the child. However, it may be that either teacher would behave in one of the two ways, depending on which children are playing with the tower blocks; that is, some children may need more help than others in attaining self-regulation.

Having a conception of children as *potentially* self-regulational permits a range of teacher interventions geared to the child's behavior. A different way of saying this is that self-regulation is, in part, learned behavior. Some children who come to us have had much experience with self-regulation and are ready to take responsibility for their own learning. Others need help in this area and, at least initially, require considerable teacher direction.

I learned this lesson the hard way. When we first started the Mt. Hope School, a lab school at the University of Rochester, I wanted the children to begin immediately setting their own work schedules. They could not. They came from settings where decisions were made for them, and they were not ready to take responsibility for their own learning. We now start the year very tightly indeed. The children even have to ask to go to the toilet or for a drink of water. Gradually we ease up as the children begin to internalize the rules and the controls. By the end of the year, children are working very much on their own.

I think that I do not disparage Montessori when I say that she may have overemphasized the "nature" of the child and underemphasized the significance of social conditioning. In effect, modern biology and genetics teach us that not one but many child "natures" exist. Which one appears depends upon the environment in which the child is reared. What Montessori recognized as the "nature" of the child was, in fact, perhaps the most fortunate and healthy expression of the child's norm of reaction.

A child's behavior, then, is not a fixed expression of his or her genes but can change with new environmental circumstances. This fact has positive and negative implications. It means that children can learn self-regulation, but it also means that they can unlearn it. The extent of reversibility is limited, but much is possible. I hope, after this discussion, that you will not think I'm an environmentalist. I continue to believe in the importance of the child's genetic endowment, but I also recognize that what aspects of that endowment are realized depends a great deal upon the particular environment in which the child is reared.

Please understand that I am not saying that young children's time in school should be spent exclusively on self-regulational activities. Children need to learn many things in other ways. Words, not the concepts that they represent, are learned by imitation, and this learning is valuable. Rules for social interaction must also be learned by means other than self-regulated activities. In short, several different modes of learning are means available to the young child, and all of them are useful and important. I do believe, however, that in young children self-regulated activities should be emphasized to a greater extent than other learning modes.

The child as a cognitive alien

A second component of the Piagetian conception of the child is that she or he is a *cognitive alien.* Young children do not think in the same way that adults do, and this is not wrong or bad; it is simply different, or alien. Let me illustrate. Recently one of the guinea pigs at the Mt. Hope school died. The children were upset, and the teacher helped them deal with their feelings by having a funeral and burying the guinea pig in a shady part of the lawn. Many of the children (seven to nine years of age) wrote notes to the animal, hoping that it would not be lonely and that it would hurry back. They lacked the adult understanding of death. Their concept of death as a temporary state is foreign to us, just as our idea of death as a permanent termination is foreign to them.

Recognition that the child is a cognitive alien carries with it the implication that the child speaks a foreign language. Certainly children use English words and grammar, but they also create their own words (like calling an attaché case "Daddy's work purse," or a moustache a "mouth brow") and use words differently than adults do. In this regard the child is also a linguistic alien. Like a person from a foreign land, children make mistakes with language and interpret it differently than do adults.

From a practical, classroom point of view, the concept of the child as a cognitive and linguistic alien has important implications. Basically, it means that *we cannot take anything for granted insofar as the child's knowledge or understanding is concerned.* In my experience this is the single most difficult rule for teachers to acquire and, once acquired, to abide by. Failure to follow this rule is perhaps the most important cause of ineffective teaching practice.

These strong statements warrant some amplification and elaboration. In no way do I mean that we should underestimate or undervalue the child's very real intellectual abilities or knowledge, nor do I mean that we have to talk down to children or be condescending to them. Quite the contrary. What I do mean is that we should relate to children as we would to intelligent individuals from another country. We have to work hard to find out what they know, how they understand things, to establish a basis of communication and to learn where to begin teaching.

I should say, parenthetically, that the tendency to take for granted what the learner knows and understands is not limited to early childhood and primary school teachers. I have sat in on many college courses in which the professors were teaching economics or statistics or something else, and I was sure they were assuming too much about the knowledge and understanding of their students. The teacher's failure to assess students' level of understanding before proceeding to teach amounts to a kind of *instructional egocentrism*–a tendency to teach material without ascertaining whether the student is ready or prepared to learn that material.

The idea of finding out where children are before intervening is as much Montessori as it is Piaget. What impresses me most when I read Montessori, perhaps because it reflects my own bias, is how she always puts the child first and method second. Our natural tendency, however, seems to be to reverse those priorities. Again and again we put the need for new methods ahead of careful observation of the child. *The price of effective teaching is constant observation.* If we learn to put children first and method second, then we won't take children's knowledge and understanding for granted.

The child as a logical thinker

If the first task of the teacher is to observe children, then how does one go about this in ways that are useful for instruction? In this domain another component of Piaget's conception of the child—namely, the child as a *logical thinker*–can be of service. In observing young children we can take our cues from Montessori and our theory from Piaget. Montessori observed children as they interacted with the materials she made available, and she gave accurate and detailed descriptions of the sequences children followed in using materials. She observed, for example, that children wrote before they read and that they read posters and signs before they read books. She used these observations as clues to teaching sequences.

Although Piaget's conception of children's thinking cannot add to the observations that Montessori made nor to those made by the contemporary teacher, his conception can provide a fuller understanding of the behavior observed. I do not disparage Montessori when I say that, to use a linguistic analogy, she observed *surface structure*, the observable sequence of behaviors, whereas Piaget sought the *deep structures*, the underlying logical abilities that determine and regulate children's surface behavior.

Let me give just a couple of examples of how deep structure interacts with surface structure to illustrate what a Piagetian analysis might add to a Montessorian observation. Consider the child who is following the teacher's example of sorting like forms into piles but arranges the different forms into a circle rather than into separate piles, one for each type of form. How shall we interpret that behavior? Montessori might conclude, correctly, that such arrangements precede correct sorting. Piaget would add that correct sorting presupposes mental operations that allow the child to mentally grasp that one and the same form can be both an individual form and a member of a class of forms. The child who builds a "graphic collection" rather than a series of piles of different forms reflects her or his tendency to group according to some perceptual form rather than according to a conceptual classification.

What the deep-structure understanding of classroom observations permits, and what the surface-structure observations do not, is *generalization.* If we know that a child cannot sort according to form, then we know that he has a general problem with the one and the many that is likely to appear in a variety of different ways that can be anticipated. For example, if this child were asked, for example, to say whether there were more boys or more children in the room, we could predict that he would say that "there are more boys than girls." The deep-structure problem here is exactly the same as in sorting according to form. In both instances the child has to see that one thing can belong to more than one class. In sorting according to form, the child has to see that a red square is both red and square. In classifying, the child has to grasp that a person can be classified as a child or as a boy or girl.

One more example: Suppose a child successfully constructs a pink tower with all of the blocks

in a correct size arrangement. What does this tell us about the child's understanding of size relations? On the surface it tells us that she grasps *ordinal numbers,* the sort of numbers assigned to cakes at a bake sale or to photographs at an exhibition. The numbers suggest rank orders but say nothing about the distance between ranks. The photograph ranked first is not twice as good as the photograph ranked second. Rankings tell us nothing about the extent of difference between the items ranked.

Suppose, however, that we want to know whether the child also has a conception of

interval numbers, of numbers used to designate not only ranks but also equal differences between ranks. This is important because the concept of interval numbers is a necessary prerequisite to all mathematical computation—addition and subtraction involve the concept of interval numbers. To test for interval-number comprehension, we need additional materials, namely, a set of blocks intermediate in size to those in the pink tower. When this second set of blocks is added, the tower will be twice as high because each new block fits between two of the original ones.

After a child has completed the first pink tower, we give her the second set of blocks and ask that these new blocks be added to make the tower higher. Many children who succeed with the initial pink tower will not be able to add the additional blocks. To add additional blocks to an existing tower requires that children recognize that one block is both smaller than the one below it and bigger than the one above it. Children who cannot add the new blocks lack an interval concept of number and probably should not be involved in computational activities. Children who correctly add the new blocks show that they have an interval conception of number and hence are ready for numerical computation.

In these examples I have tried to show how Montessori's emphasis on observing the child interacting with materials can be coupled with a Piagetian analysis of the deep structure of the behavior. The value of deep-structure analysis is that it permits generalization beyond the immediate task and suggests the presence or absence of abilities required to interact with a variety of materials. Accordingly, Piaget's conception of the child as a logical thinker adds a new dimension to the kinds of observations of children that Montessori taught us to make.

I must make one other point in connection with the deep-structure analysis of behavior. As I have suggested in the case of number, one concept can be understood at many different levels. Unfortunately our language does not always provide designations for these levels of conceptualization. The term *reading* is a good example. Being able to recognize a few words by sight requires quite different abilities than does reading with decoding and comprehension, yet often both activities are called "reading," with no attempt to distinguish the different processes that underlie these apparently similar surface behaviors.

Just as two children who correctly assemble the pink tower may have different levels of understanding number, two children able to "read" a few words may have different underlying skills and capacities. In looking at behavior from a Piagetian perspective, therefore, we must always ask about the structures that lie beneath the behavior. We must also be cautious with language and qualify our descriptions by saying, for example, that the child has the concept of "ordinal" number or a "sight" vocabulary rather than that he "knows his numbers and can read." Many controversies in education are empty because the contenders on either side use the same words for different skills or different words for the same skill.

The child as emotional compatriot

The fourth component of the Piagetian conception of the child has to do with the affective domain. If the child is a cognitive alien, then she or he is also an *emotional compatriot*. Put differently, children are least like adults in their thoughts and most like us in their feelings. Unfortunately we often turn that premise on its head, both with adult aliens and with children. Tales of the "ugly American" abroad are legendary. People behave abroad as they never would at home. One reason is that Americans abroad assume that foreigners don't have the same feelings and needs that Americans have. On the cognitive plane, however, they assume that everyone does, or should, know English and should immediately understand their questions and demands.

Something similar happens when adults deal with children. Adults often expect children to understand all that they say but not to share the same feelings. I recall taking my son, Paul, to a pediatrician for a shot. The doctor came in, and without saying a word, he looked at the chart and began to swab Paul's arm preparatory to an injection. I intervened and told him that he could not give the boy a shot without talking to him and explaining what he was doing. He then took the trouble to talk to Paul and to explain why he was giving the shot and that it would only hurt for a minute. I am sure that if the doctor were giving a shot to an adult, he would have said more than he did to my then–six-year-old son.

In education this tendency to view children's feelings as different from our own appears in a rather peculiar way. It appears as a separation between thinking and feeling or between cognitive and affective education. We have a number of "affective curricula," such as value clarification and reality therapy.

Whatever these programs' proponents originally intended, in fact the programs are often understood to be something that is appended to existing curricula. The implication is that when children are working at reading or math or social studies, they are engaged in cognitive activities, but when they are engaged in, say, value clarification, they are involved in affective activities. For children, then, we assume a sharp separation exists between thinking activities and feeling activities.

We make no such separation for ourselves. How many times have we told ourselves or others, "I'm too emotionally involved to be objective about this situation," meaning that our thinking is colored by our emotions. The close relation between feeling and thought is apparent anywhere we look. We feel good if we solve a problem or finish a job and feel bad when we do not. What often moves us on to do boring work is the anticipation of the pleasure to be produced by the end result of the work, whether it be money or a product.

We need not belabor the point. From a Piagetian perspective, thinking and feeling are simply different facets of the same ongoing behavior. The child who is busy reading or writing in the classroom is not an encapsulated thinking machine; far from it. Children work at school mainly for social rewards, at least initially. In any case, most thinking, if not all, has a motivating force behind it; this means that thinking is inextricably bound to feeling. We need to be careful, then, that the notion of affective education does not mislead us into viewing thinking and feeling as separate processes.

If we turn now to the implications of this view for classroom teaching, we can see the basic error of so-called affective education programs. Too often, as I have said, affective education is seen as adding a *new* and *different* mode of interaction, but if thinking always involves feelings, then all teacher–child interactions involve feelings, and our aim should be to change *existing* interactions in a positive direction.

In my opinion, therefore, we do not need special affective education programs. What we do need are preservice and in-service teacher-training programs designed to give teachers a better understanding of child development. Affective education programs were devised because, apparently, children displayed unhappy or unresolved feelings in the classroom. But don't such feelings arise at least in part from the teacher's conception of the child? If a teacher sees children as like herself in thinking but not in feeling, how will that teacher treat children? If the children do not learn what they are supposed to learn, the teacher will assume that they are not motivated or that they are dumb or that they are learning disabled. The responsibility for learning is laid on the children because the teacher assumes that they understand what they have to do and are refusing, for one reason or another, to do it. The teacher communicates this attitude to children, and they react with frustration and anger. At the heart of the affective interaction between teacher and child, then, is the teacher's conception of the child.

That is why I believe that affective education as a separate entity is unnecessary. Consider the teacher who assumes that children are like him or her in feelings but not in thoughts, and who believes that children are self-regulational. Such a teacher will not take for granted what a child knows and will make efforts to understand where the child is and what materials are appropriate. The teacher who operates in this way communicates feelings of warmth, of caring, and of respect for the young person, and young people respond with similar feelings. In my view, such a teacher–child relationship is the most worthwhile affective education of all.

To be sure, teachers can learn to use useful techniques and procedures in certain conflict situations, but these techniques and procedures will be transformed by the teacher's conception of the child. The best way to train teachers to be more effective with children is not by giving them more procedures and techniques but rather by giving them new insights into how children think and feel. The teacher's conception of the child is the most powerful determinant of the nature of the teacher–child affective interaction. That is why, to my mind, acquiring the Piagetian conception of the child is even more important for teachers than acquiring specific methods and techniques.

Summary

I have suggested that classroom practice is always dictated by the teacher's conception of the child. Coupling a comparison of Montessorian and Piagetian-based classroom practices with a description of the Piagetian conception of the child was therefore necessary. From this standpoint the child is viewed, first, as *potentially self-regulational*–capable of learning in a directed, organized, and self-correcting way. Self-regulated behavior, however, is but one of the many possible expressions of child "nature," and the extent to which a child engages in it is, at least in part, a matter of environmental input.

From a Piagetian standpoint the child is also a *cognitive alien*, a person who thinks differently than adults do and who uses language in a different way. Holding this view of children requires that we take nothing for granted as to what children know and understand and that we take the time to find out where children are in their learning and capabilities before we commence teaching.

Finding out where children are can be helped by a third component of the Piagetian conception of the child, namely, the child as a *logical thinker*. Piaget's description of the logical structures presupposed by different tasks adds a new dimension to classroom observation and allows generalization and prediction from one type of behavior to another.

Finally, Piaget suggests that children are *emotional compatriots* in the sense that they share the same needs and feelings that we do. Because feelings are but the other side of cognitions, we do not need affective curricula that are added on to existing curricula; rather, what is needed, if problems exist, are *changes* in the way teachers interact with children. If teachers learn to see children as potentially self-regulational, as requiring effort to be understood, as being logical thinkers, and as possessing feelings and needs as adults do, then the teacher will convey an attitude of respect toward the children. This attitude of respect will be reciprocated by the children, who will learn to respect others as well as themselves. This is the best affective education of all.

In conclusion, then, the way in which we work with young people is always colored by our implicit assumptions about the nature of children. I am not advocating that everyone adopt the Piagetian position in this respect; diversity is beneficial to growth. I am saying that if someone decides he wants to apply Piagetian principles in the classroom, he must first understand and accept the conception of the child from which those principles are derived.

The original version of this essay based on a 1977 invited address to the American Montessori Association meeting in Philadelphia, appeared in *The Child and Society* (pp. 143–155) by David Elkind, 1979, New York: Oxford University Press. Used with permission.

Work Is Hardly Child's Play

The role of play in human development has been interpreted and understood in many different ways and from the perspectives of several quite different disciplines. A comprehensive list of the many divergent approaches to the origin of play has been offered by Bruner, Jolly, and Sylva (1976). The focus of this chapter is much more limited and attempts to compare and contrast the writings of Montessori, Erikson, and Piaget, with respect to their positions on play. Their theories have a common bond because Erikson was trained as a Montessori teacher, and the Maison des Petits, the Lab School at Piaget's Institute in Geneva where much of Piaget's early research was done, had a modified Montessori program.

In addition to this theoretical connection, an applied connection exits. Although none of the three were educators by profession

(Montessori was a physician, Erikson gave up teaching for psychoanalysis, and Piaget is a psychologist), all three have had a considerable impact upon educational practice, particularly at the early childhood level.

Maria Montessori

In 1896 Maria Montessori received her degree in medicine in Italy. She was just 26 years old and the first woman physician in that country. After achieving some remarkable results working with retarded children, she was given the task of rehabilitating a group of "slum" children in a child care center serving a housing development in a poor section of Rome. There she began evolving the educational theories and practice that have since won her worldwide recognition.

A tribute to Montessori, perhaps the highest tribute that can be paid to an innovator, is that many of her concepts and methods have become part of established educational practice and are no longer associated with her name. Use of child-sized chairs and tables, the concept of a "prepared" environment suited to the child's level of cognitive ability, and ample provision of manipulative materials from which children can learn basic concepts all derive from Montessori.

One Montessori contribution has not become assimilated into early childhood educational practice, however—her conception of play. To this day, the greatest divergence between Montessori and non-Montessori child-centered classrooms resides in how each handles play and fantasy. What made this Montessori conception so unattractive when so much else of her approach was swiftly taken over by those working with young children?

Play as the child's work

First of all, although Montessori was a revolutionary in an educational sense, she was not a revolutionary in a political sense. She saw education, good education, as the best means by which children become good citizens of high character. To be sure, she advocated that children should be appreciated and respected as persons in their own right, and she expected that such treatment would result in adults who were self-respecting as well. The thrust of her educational method, however, was social adaptation. The value of teaching at the child's level was that the child could learn the basic skills of the culture. Her image of the child was as an immigrant "who goes to a new country ignorant of its products, ignorant of its natural appearance and social order, entirely ignorant of its language," confronted with "an immense work of adaptation which he must perform before he can associate himself with the active life of the unknown people" (Montessori, 1965, p. 35).

Montessori's conception of play was also grounded in the contemporary thinking of her time. Carlotta Lombroso, a prominent 19th-century philosopher of education, wrote, "Play is for the child an occupation as serious, as important, as study is for the adult; play is in his means of development and he needs to play, just as the silkworm needs continually to eat leaves" (1896, p. 117). Likewise, Karl Groos argued that "the animal does not play because he is young, rather he has a period of youth because he must play" (1901). From this standpoint play is the natural and essential activity of the young in preparation for adult life.

The conception of play that was in vogue when Montessori wrote was that play is the natural activity of the child and that its function is to prepare the child for adult life. Montessori wedded this conception to her view of education as social adaptation when she wrote that "Play is the child's work." In fact, she went much further than did Groos. To Groos, play serves as a socializing force in the sense of modulating instincts, but the modulation of instincts gives rise to art and personal expression as well as social adaptation. This dimension of play, its artistic and aesthetic dimension, was somehow lost in Montessori's presentation. Stated simply, play to Montessori has little value in and of itself and takes on importance only when it is used for socialization.

Montessori's emphasis on the use of play and fantasy for social adaptation rather than for artistic personal expression is shown in the following paragraph.

Imagination has always been given a predominant place in the psychology of childhood, and all over the world people tell their children fairy stories which are enjoyed immensely, as if the children wanted to exercise this great gift, as imagination undoubtedly is.

But then she adds,

Yet when all are agreed that a child loves to imagine, why do we give him only fairy tales and toys on which to practice his gift? If a child can imagine a fairy and fairyland, it will not be difficult for him to imagine America. Instead of hearing it vaguely in conversation, he can help to clarify his own ideas of it by looking at the globe on which it is shown. (Montessori, 1967, p. 177)

As suggested here, Montessori regarded fairy tales as frivolous and believed that the child's imagination could be put to better use learning about the real world.

Why did this gifted woman, who had such brilliant insights into children and their ways of thinking and feeling, eschew the aesthetic, the personal, the artistic side of children and of children's play? This question would certainly provoke an interesting psychohistorical investigation. My guess is that the aesthetic was not important to Montessori personally or was not something she took great pleasure in. One gets very little sense of aesthetic appreciation in her books. On the other hand, she was enormously productive and achievement oriented. In short, Montessori's view of play as social adaptation may have come from her personal value system rather than from her observation of children. Perhaps that is why her conception of play has been less accepted than many of her other contributions.

Erik Erikson

Erik Erikson was a student of Freud's as well as of Montessori's, and his conception of play bears traces of both of his teachers as well as his own unique genius. In 1896 when Montessori received her medical degree, Sigmund Freud had turned away from neurology and began his investigations of psychoneuroses. In 1895 he and Joseph Breuer first published their classic *Studies in Hysteria* (Breuer & Freud, 1937), and in 1904 Freud published *The Interpretation of Dreams* (1938).

Not surprisingly, Freud shared the conception of play as a kind of work. In *The Interpretation of Dreams*, for example, he spoke of "dream work," by which he meant the mental processes that transform unacceptable, unconscious wishes and impulses into acceptable, if often undecipherable, conscious dream images. Dream work clearly has an adaptive function: it allows a person to sleep undisturbed by wishes and impulses that, if they were known, would awaken and distress the person.

In children's fantasy and play, one can see in operation the same mechanisms that we see in dreams—displacement, condensation, and substitution. An analyst would say, for example, that in block play a child may substitute blocks for people, displace feelings when she or he knocks the blocks over, and condense many different life themes into a particular form of play. Play work is thus parallel to dream work.

The Freudian identification of play and work, however, is of a different order than the identification made by Montessori. First, to Montessori, as to other psychologists such as Koffka (1927), play was the dominant mode of child behavior; the child was by nature a playing creature. What Montessori argued was that this play is not, or at least should not be, frivolous. Play should be in the service of social adaptation.

Freud, however, distinguished between primary and secondary process thought, and he recognized that children were capable of both. Primary process thought includes the processes of dream work, while secondary process thought is logical and mathematical. Freud, therefore, recognized two types of adaptation and two types of adaptive processes. One type of adaptation is directed toward the pleasure-seeking instincts and is called the *pleasure principle*. A second type of adaptation is directed toward the external world and is called the *reality principle*.

Freud thus differed from Montessori in two major respects. First, children are not totally engaged in play because they operate according to the reality principle as well as the pleasure principle. Second, while play involves effort in the sense that it is an adaptation, it is not social adaptation, at least not directly. Play, from a psychodynamic viewpoint, has less to do with mastery of the world than with mastery of the self. Play is the means by which we are able to control our inner forces that threaten established social relations. Accordingly, Montessori said that children's play is subordinate to work, whereas Freud said that children's work (primary process work) is subordinate to play.

This view of play extends to wit and humor as well. Jokes, from a Freudian position, always have a sexual or an aggressive content. Like dreams they permit the expression of unacceptable impulses in nonthreatening ways. Laughter is the release of a hidden reservoir of tension built up from repressed anger and sexual impulses and feelings. So we laugh for the same reason that we play: we are able to express in acceptable, if disguised, ways our deep-seated conflicts, anxieties, and wishes.

Integrating Montessori and Freud

Erikson attempted to integrate the Montessori and the Freudian positions. The desire to integrate diverse positions, to create an ordered whole or an identity, is characteristic of Erikson's work. He would be the first to acknowledge that his concern with the integration of apparently unrelated or contradictory conceptions stems from his own efforts to construct a unified whole from the disparate parts of his own profession and personal background.

In the chapter "Toys and Reasons" in *Childhood and Society* (1950), Erikson makes explicit his conception of play and how it differs from that of Freud and the psychoanalysts. He offers the passage from *Tom Sawyer* in which Tom is starting to whitewash the fence and one of his friends appears. Ben Rogers, the friend, is imitating a steamboat, its captain, and its crew. Erikson asks how this sort of imaginative play is to be interpreted and offers in response some typical psychoanalytic explanations he received from a class of social workers he was teaching. Their answers suggested that Ben Rogers was expressing and working through some family trauma, such as an overbearing father or bed-wetting.

Erikson, in contrast, offers an explanation epitomized in the statement, "Ben is a growing boy." Erikson writes,

To grow means to be divided into different parts which move at different rates. A growing boy has trouble in mastering his gangling body as

well as his divided mind. He wants to be good, if only out of expediency, and always finds that he has been bad. He wants to rebel, and finds that almost against his will, he has given in. As his time perspective permits a glimpse of approaching adulthood, he finds himself acting like a child. One "meaning" of Ben's play could be that it affords his ego a temporary victory over his gangling body and self by making a well functioning whole out of brain (captain), the nerves and muscles of will (signal system and engine) and the whole bulk of the body (boat). It permits him to be an entity within which he is his own boss because he obeys himself. (1950, p. 211)

For Erikson, therefore, play has a much broader function than it did for Freud. Play is not just an outlet for dangerous wishes and impulses; it can also be a means, a symbolic tool, for coping with the normal asynchronies and contradictions inherent in mental and physical growth. Ben's play, to put it simply, was an expression of health, not of illness. Although play can have curative powers for children suffering from emotional disturbance, it goes beyond that function.

Growing up in a particular society at a particular time in history and in a particular ethnic milieu presents every individual with problems of adaptation that are part of his or her human condition. Not all of a young person's conflicts derive from disturbances in childrearing, and some conflicts are evidence of growth and adaptation to particular social circumstances. Play, then, cannot be reduced to an expression of familial trauma and must be seen more broadly as symbolizing many different facets of a child's growth and problems of adaptation to self and social milieu.

While one can applaud this broadening conception of child's play, it is less easy to applaud Erikson's slip back to the Montessori identification of work and play, of social adaptation and personal expression. Oddly enough, after showing the value of play as personal expression in Ben Rogers's case, Erikson concludes with the following sentence:

At the same time, he chooses his metaphors from the tool world of the young machine age, and anticipates the identity of the machine God of the day, the captain of the Big Missouri.

Play is social adaptation as well as personal expression. That Erikson intends this identification of work and play is clear from his use of an anthropological (American Indian) example from Ruth Underhill that sounds a lot like Montessori:

The man of the house turned to his little three-year-old granddaughter and asked her to close the door. The door was heavy and hard to shut. The child tried but it did not move. Several times the grandfather repeated, "Yes, close the door." No one jumped to the child's assistance. No one took the responsibility away from her. On the other hand there was no impatience because the child was small. They sat gravely waiting until the child succeeded and her grandfather thanked her. It was assumed that the task would not be asked of her unless she could perform it, and having been asked, the responsibility was hers alone, just as if she were a grown woman. (1950, p. 236)

Erikson argues that this child is conditioned to social participation early with tasks geared to her level of ability. In American society, he argues, this is not the case, and children are not treated as equals with adults until at least adolescence. And he concludes,

It dawns on us then, that the theories of play which are advanced in our culture and which take as their foundation the assumption that in children too, play is defined by the fact that it is not work, are really one of the many prejudices by which we exclude our children from an early source of a sense of identity. (1950, p. 237)

According to Erikson the separation of work and play in childhood is a "prejudice"; hence, we are back to Montessori by way of Freud. Montessori argues that play is social adaptation, whereas Freud argues that it reflects personal adaptation. Erikson extends

Freud's notion to show that play could be an expression of personal growth as well as personal conflict, but then Erikson gives up the important distinction between the individual and the social and argues that this distinction is a prejudice. He says that separating personal adaptation from social adaptation in our society would be regrettable. Apparently, for Erikson, children attain a healthier sense of ego identity in a society in which play is a child's work than in one in which these two activities are separate.

Jean Piaget

Piaget was born in 1896, the same year that Montessori became a doctor of medicine and a year after the publication of Breuer and Freud's *Studies in Hysteria*. Piaget was thus of a different generation than the other two investigators, although he was greatly influenced by them. This influence, however, was tempered by a healthy skepticism grounded in an empirical mentality. Piaget was unwilling to accept what others said about the development of child life without first checking what they proposed against his own observations and analytical evaluation.

In this mode Piaget attacked the problem of children's play (1963). He was extraordinarily well read in this field, as in other fields that he investigated, and his challenges to the theory of Karl Groos (1901) and those of Claparede, Piaget's mentor (1946), were based on a solid understanding of those positions. Indeed, Piaget often saw broader implications in a writer's theory than the writer had seen.

Piaget set himself three major tasks, the basic ones of scientific inquiry. He first sought to classify play behavior, regarding classification as the first and essential step in any scientific investigation. Second, he attempted to describe the rules that operate in the development of these behaviors. And third, he sought a general explanation of these behaviors, based on general principles of human development. Piaget's work on play, although begun in his first exploratory stage of his career, was completed during his second period, when he sought to trace the origins of intelligence to the sensorimotor coordination of infants. More specifically, his aim was to explain play in terms of its place in the evolution of intelligence.

Piaget argued that classifications based on content (such as sensorial, motor, or intellectual games) or on functions (such as fighting, counting, or family games) were bound to be inconsistent and inadequate. Such classifications reflect only superficial differences, while a classification based on *deep structure*, to borrow a term from linguist Noam Chomsky (1957), groups play behaviors on the basis of underlying structural differences.

Three types of play

Using this type of analysis and his meticulous observations of his own three infants as his primary data, Piaget distinguished three types of play: *practice play, symbolic play*, and *games with rules*. Practice play occurs during the first few months of life and can be observed whenever the child acts for the sake of acting. An infant who sucks his thumb or grasps and lets go of an object is engaged in practice play. What characterizes this activity and why it is play, in Piaget's conception, is that it is almost entirely *assimilative*. Assimilation always involves a transformation of experience in the service of the self. The infant who is sucking her thumb has transformed that thumb into an object to be sucked. She has transformed the object to meet personal needs.

In Piaget's view practice play is usually short lived and generally appears after mastery of some type of sensorimotor coordination. It reappears throughout childhood whenever the child acquires a new skill. At the same time the child is engaging in practice play, however, he is also engaging in imitation. Through imitation the child begins to be able to represent objects and to differentiate words from the objects they signify. At about age two this distinction becomes fully operative, and the child becomes capable of representing his experience at a temporal and spatial distance from it. The delayed reaction, or the child's ability to respond to a hidden object after a time delay, is an example of this capability.

After about age two until age four or five, children are primarily engaged in representational activities. These activities move in two directions: One is toward conventional representations, concepts, verbal signs, and the socialization of experience; the other is toward distorted representations, symbols, and the expression of personal feelings and conflicts. The preschool child is learning signs and becoming socialized, but he or she is also creating symbols that reflect individuality.

Piaget, like Freud, thus distinguishes between work and play in early childhood. The young child is working and accommodating—transforming the self to meet the demands of the world—much of the time. She or he is told not to get dirty, to say please, to eat more slowly, to talk more clearly, and so on. At the same time, children engage in symbolic play that is really not accommodative. Boys and girls playing house and store are really not only modeling adult roles. Symbolic play is not merely imitative; it has many transformational components, such as endowing dolls with life and empty cups with coffee. Such play reflects personal needs for mastery and control and is not primarily social adaptation.

The critical distinguishing feature of symbolic play in young children, then, is not its function nor its imitative components but rather the presence of symbols. For Piaget a symbol is a personal representation, as opposed to a sign, which is a conventional, social representation. Because children are far from mastering the complex world of signs and the concepts these represent, children need symbols to represent their personal needs and conflicts. For Piaget symbolic play is important in its own right as a necessary means for dealing with wishes, desires, and conflicts by one who is not completely socialized and thus does not have socialized means of expression and conflict resolution.

As children attain concrete operations—the ability to engage in syllogistic reasoning—at about age six or seven, symbolic play diminishes in frequency and is replaced with games with rules. Social play gradually replaces individual play, and socially constructed game rules replace personally constructed symbols. Game rules, in Piaget's view, are collective symbols in the sense that they still distort reality and yet are shared by several individuals. Games with rules can be handed down by oral tradition, as in the case of marbles and jacks, or can be made up by a group of children, as in spontaneously tossing around a child's hat to keep him from getting it.

To Piaget the appearance of games with rules brings about a diminution of egocentrism and a new level of social integration. In his view, as a consequence of the maturing child's increasing size and competencies, he or she finds other, socialized avenues for expressing personal needs or wishes. In games with rules, for example, the child can express competitive needs in a socially prescribed way. More generally, play, in the pure sense of assimilation unmodified by accommodation, becomes increasingly less common as children grow older and become socialized beings.

Piaget does not deny, of course, that some form of symbolic activity still goes on in later life. Dreams and fantasy are examples because they reflect distorting assimilation, but even dreams and fantasies are far more socialized in the older child and in the adult than they are in early childhood. The majority of the child's play activity—and the adult's, for that matter—is socialized and reflects a healthy integration of the personal and the social. Of course, numerous exceptions to this general rule exist. Some people are poor losers and cannot treat a game as a game.

Implications of Piaget's view of play

In reviewing this discussion of Piaget's theory of play, we can derive an education implication. Piaget alludes to children's artistic expression and personal scientific preoccupations becoming more socialized during childhood. Children begin to draw in much more conventionalized ways, and individual collections, such as teddy bears, give way to social collections such as coins, stamps, and comic books, which are traded from one young person to another.

Although Piaget does not emphasize it, I believe that the socialization of these two facets of play reveals the beginnings of art and science. Both art and science provide a unique integration of the personal and the social. Good art is at once personal and social and provides a unique vision of the world that can nonetheless be shared and enjoyed by others. The artist, in a sense, creates collective symbols through which many can express their personal feeling and desires. The scientist does the same thing in a somewhat different way; she or he creates a new concept that allows others to see the world in new ways.

Science and art, therefore, grow out of the separation between work and play in early childhood. Indeed, I propose that the tension between play and work, between personal expression and social accommodation, is essential for their later integration. For that reason I oppose the equating of work and play in early childhood, and I urge that young children have the opportunity to play as well as work.

Summary and conclusion

Montessori equated work and play in early childhood inasmuch as she argued that play should be put in the service of social adaptation. Erikson, who was a student of Montessori's but also of Freud's, attempted to reconcile the Freudian theory of play as a kind of personal catharsis with the Montessorian notion that play should be social adaptation. Erikson suggested that play can express healthy growth processes and need not always be a disguised expression of hidden impulses. Yet he also argued that play was a means of relating to one's culture and argued that the distinction between work and play in childhood is a prejudice.

Piaget takes a developmental perspective on play and sees it as having different forms at different age levels. In infants one sees a form of practice play, in which action is repeated for the sense of function pleasure and in which accommodation is subordinate to assimilation. In the preschool period, thanks to the construction of personal symbols, assimilation becomes differentiated from accommodative activities, and symbolic play becomes the means by which the child expresses unsocialized desires and impulses. In childhood, assimilation and accommodation, play and work, are reconciled in games with rules. Such games are social inasmuch as they involve mutual obligations, but they are also personal because they involve individual competitiveness. In addition, games involve collective symbols—distorted representations of the world. In marbles, for example, the glass balls can represent different things to different children. They are collective because they are shared and personal because they have no specific shared meaning other than their role in the game.

I have argued that the distinction between work and play in early childhood—advocated by Freud and Piaget, opposed by Montessori and Erikson—is important and should be maintained. I believe that this distinction is really not a cultural prejudice, as Erikson suggests. Vygtosky (1978), writing from a Marxist perspective, describes play (the subordination of the object to the meaning) and work (the subordination of the meaning to the object) in terms similar to Piaget's. The distinction between play and work, between personal assimilation and social accommodations, is important because it provides the necessary tension for the kinds of integration that we call science and art. Good art, like good science, is a unique integration between the particular and the universal, between what is unique to the individual and what is common to mankind.

Recognition of the distinction between work and play is really recognition of our biological heritage. Each of us has a unique combination of genes that will never be repeated, but we also have the same number of chromosomes at the same loci as everyone else. We are like everyone else but different, too. At its simplest level, then, play and work reflect our existential dilemma of being both one and many. Denying or ignoring this dilemma is, as I have argued here, a mistake because the distinction provides the tension out of which man's lasting achievements emerge. More particularly, in young children we should encourage play for its own sake because it provides an avenue for children to express themselves in personal ways. Paradoxical as it may seem, personal expression in early childhood may be the best possible preparation for social accommodation later. Play is not the child's work, and work is hardly child's play.

References

Breuer, J., & Freud, S. (1937). *Studies in hysteria.* Boston: Beacon Press.

Bruner, J., Jolly, A., & Sylva, K. (Eds.). (1976). *Play: Its role in development and evolution.* New York: Penguin.

Chomsky, N. (1957). *Syntactic structures.* The Hague: Mouton.

Claparede, E. (1946). *Education functionelle.* Neuchátel: Delachaux.

Erikson, E. (1950). *Childhood and society.* New York: Norton.

Freud, S. (1938). The interpretation of dreams. In *The basic writings of Sigmund Freud* (pp. 181–549). New York: Modern Library.

Groos, K. (1901). *The play of man.* New York: Appleton.

Koffka, K. (1927). *The growth of the mind: An introduction to child psychology.* New York: Harcourt Brace.

Lombroso, C. (1896). L'instinct de la conservation chez les enfants. Rev. Philos. XLIII, 379–390.

Montessori, M. (1965). *Dr. Montessori's own handbook.* New York: Schocken. (Original work published 1914)

Montessori, M. (1967). *The absorbent mind.* New York: Delta.

Piaget, J. (1963). *Play, dreams and imitation in childhood.* New York: Norton.

Vygotsky, L.S. (1978). *Mind in society.* Cambridge, MA: Harvard University Press.

The original version of this essay appeared in *Children and Adolescents: Interpretive Essays on Jean Piaget* (3rd. Ed.) (pp. 188–202) by David Elkind, 1981. New York: Oxford University Press. Used with permission.

Development in Early Childhood

hildren three and four years of age make significant progress in their intellectual, social, and emotional development in a relatively short period of time. However, it is often easy to misread this progress and to assume that young children are more mature and more competent than they really are. As I have emphasized in my writing (Elkind, 1987, 1988), overestimating young children's competence can lead to hurrying and to miseducation, both of which are stressful to the child. In many cases, the stress from hurrying and miseducating children is intense enough to necessitate the counseling of young children and their families.

Accordingly, in this article I review some of the major cognitive, social, and emotional achievements of young children and also some of their limitations. By outlining these limitations I in no way intend to demean or belittle young children's capacities. They make enormous progress in a few short years, but they still have a long way to go to reach maturity. To recognize their limitations as well as their strengths is only to emphasize their humanness and their unique place in the human life cycle.

First, the description of development as divided into intellectual, language, social, and emotional development is necessary for organized presentation. These terms represent adult categories of thought, not distinct modes of thought and action in the child. For young children, all of these processes and abilities are of a piece. A young child's intellectual and verbal abilities are part and parcel of one another, as are the child's social and emotional interactions and expressions. Although we discuss these processes and abilities separately, we must remember that they are far from separate in the life of the actively engaged young child.

Intellectual abilities

Preoperations

By three or four years old, children have attained what Piaget (1950) called functions, or "preoperations," that enable them to perform a number of feats far beyond the capabilities of infants. Infants concentrate on constructing a world of permanent objects; once constructed, these objects will exist for the infant even when they are no longer present to his or her senses. Preschool children, in contrast, are constructing a world of qualities and properties that different objects have in common. They are beginning to identify and name colors, shapes, textures, density, and so on. At this stage, children are beginning to understand *same* and *different* as these terms refer to properties.

These new abilities are easy to observe when children are playing at home or in a child care setting. At this age, children can sort buttons according to color and correctly place differently shaped pieces into geometric and nongeometric form boards. They also begin to recognize and name certain animals, cars, and pieces of furniture, and many different types of food. At this stage, then, children have the capacity to begin organizing the world of disparate objects into a world in which many different objects fall within the same class or category.

However, we must not lose sight of the fact that these classes are formed on the basis of perceptual attributes, such as color and form, and not on the basis of any quantitative characteristics. Moreover, although children can name and identify members of different classes, such as *cow, dog,* or *car,* they cannot as yet operate on these categories in a systematic way. That is, they cannot logically add categories and recognize that cats, dogs, and cows are all animals, nor can they logically multiply classes and appreciate that a cat is

both a cat and an animal at the same time. In short, the one/many, or quantitative, dimension of classes escapes young children. Only when they have attained the concrete operations of childhood (at age six to seven years) will they begin to be able to coordinate sameness and difference and arrive at the notion of a unit that is basic to all quantitative thinking. A unit—for example, the number 3— is at once like every other number in that it is a *number* but also different in that it is the only number that comes after 2 and before 4. Once children have a notion of a unit, they can engage in numerical thought as well as logical addition and multiplication.

The young child's limitation with respect to operating on classes is most evident when we ask them to define a word. Young children routinely define words by describing their functions—an apple is *to eat;* a bike is *to ride.* Only when they attain concrete operations will they begin to define terms by nesting them in higher order classes, in which an apple is *a fruit* and a bike *has wheels–you go places with it.* Occasionally young children may define a word by placing it within a broader context, but this is often an anticipation of later intellectual achievement, not a true reflection of the young child's competence.

Learning processes

Within their limited sphere, most young children (three to five years old) can use a number of learning strategies. Young children can sort objects according to their qualities or properties; for example, they can put triangles in one box and squares in another. Young children can seriate objects according to size: a young child can correctly stack a set of size-graded plastic "donuts" on a center post. Young children can match to sample: If we give a young child a card with a picture of a tree and ask her to find the same picture among a set of pictures of different things, the child can do so with ease. Young children must have concrete experience—the geometric forms, colors, textures (smooth, soft, etc.)—in concrete manipulable materials before we give them the labels. With the concrete experience the labels have meaning; without it they are simply sounds.

Young children have excellent rote memorization skills. After young children have heard a story read to them several times, they know immediately when the adult reader has omitted a word. Young children also have perceptual memory superior to that of older children or adults. If they are asked to look at a set of pictures that are then turned over, young children can correctly identify more of the pictures than adults can. This sort of photographic memory (sometimes called "eidetic imagery") is probably a function, at least in part, of the fact that the young child's store of long-term memories is less crowded than that of older children and adults. Presumably, memory retrieval is easier when the memory banks are less crowded. Also, adults may attempt to use verbal memory strategies, which generally are less effective than simple image retention.

Variability of individual growth rates

In discussing young children's intellectual growth and abilities, it is difficult to overemphasize the wide range of normal variability in the age at which they attain their new mental powers. Describing the characteristics of the three-year-old or the four-year-old, as Gesell and his coworkers have done (Gesell, et al., 1949), is sometimes useful; however, such generalizations can be misleading. Although some temperamental characteristics are relatively unique to each age group, a great deal of intellectual variability exists among children. This individual variability has sometimes been obscured by the tendency to think of young children in terms of temperament rather than intellectual development.

Benjamin Bloom (1964) has pointed out that the preschool years are a time of extremely rapid intellectual growth. One characteristic of periods of rapid growth, intellectual or otherwise, is that they tend to exaggerate individual differences. Consider early adolescence and the growth spurt associated

with puberty (Tanner, 1961). Girls are generally taller than boys of the same age, and some boys and girls mature earlier than others. The physical variability among boys and girls in a sixth or seventh grade classroom is incredible.

Although not nearly so visible, individual differences in intellectual ability among young children are every bit as great as individual differences in physical development among teenagers. Just as most of the teenagers' growth rate differences level off by the age of 15 to 16 years, most of the individual differences in young children's ability will even out by the time the children reach third or fourth grade. In the meantime we must appreciate that much of the variability among young children in readiness to learn has to do with variability in growth rate and nothing more. We have to avoid misdiagnosing young children as learning disabled when in fact their growth pattern is such that they temporarily fall behind their peers.

Recognizing the normal variability in growth rates is particularly important today, when the academic pressures for achievement and testing have been pushed downward into kindergarten and even into prekindergarten (see, for example, Kamii, 1990). One consequence of this trend is that our perception of the range of "normality" has been compressed. Twenty years ago, for example, children of three and four years of age who did not know their letters and numbers were regarded as well within the norm of average intellectual development. Today children of that age are often targeted for remediation if they do not have this knowledge by the time they are in kindergarten.

We must therefore appreciate that a great deal of normal variation in intellectual development exists during the early childhood years. The majority of slow–growth-rate children will catch up and do just fine—provided they are given the time and manipulative materials they need to fully realize their cognitive abilities. This is less likely to happen if they are falsely labeled or singled out for special treatment.

Modes of thought

Some writers (e.g., Bryant, 1972; Donaldson, 1978; Gelman, Meck, & Merkin, 1986) have argued that Piaget focused on the limitations of young children's thinking to the exclusion of their competencies. This is far from being the case; indeed, just the opposite is true. Prior to Piaget's work, children's minds were thought to be little more than blank slates. Piaget's early work (1932; more recent editions, 1951, 1952) revealed the richness and complexity of young children's thought. He believed that in many ways the thinking of young children resembles that of the ancient Greek philosophers. Rather than demonstrating the limitations of children's thinking, Piaget revealed the hitherto unknown, hidden side of children's minds.

Young children think differently than older children and adults, but differences in levels of thought do not signal inferiority any more than do differences in culture or language.

Realism

Young children tend to believe that psychic phenomena, such as their dreams and feelings, are physical in nature and thus can be observed and felt by others. I once asked a young child who was complaining of a toothache if it hurt very much, and he replied, "Yes, can't you feel it?" Piaget found that young children also take words quite literally; for example, a young boy, whose stepmother had just given birth to a boy, was told that when he came home from nursery school that day, he would be able to see his "half brother." The boy became frightened and refused to go home—he did not want to look at half of a brother.

Animism

Young children tend to think that everything that moves is alive. Because they cannot yet understand life in the biological sense, a more complex mode of thought, they associate life with movement. A stone that is rolling down the hill is alive, as is a cloud moving across the sky. Things that do not move are dead, but they can come alive again if they move again. That is why young children will sometimes be scared by what, to the adult, seems like an innocuous cloth or leaf blowing in the wind.

Phenomenalistic causality

Understanding causality is difficult at any age, but particularly for young children, who lack experience and have limited intellectual power. Not surprisingly, young children understand causality in a rather straightforward way—specifically, that an event occurring just before another has actually caused it. A child who raises the window shade and sees the sun shining may assume that raising the shade made the sun shine. One reason that young children cling to security blankets or dolls is that these objects once brought them comfort, so the children assume that they will always do so.

The young child's phenomenalistic approach to causality helps to explain their moral judgments as well. Lacking a sense of intentionality, young children tend to judge culpability on the grounds of the amount of damage done rather than on an understanding of the perpetrator's intentions. As Piaget (1932) demonstrated, a young child will believe that a child who broke 10 cups trying to help a parent wash the dishes is more culpable than a child who broke 2 cups going after candy that his parents had told him not to touch. Only later in childhood, after children have attained new mental abilities, will they be able to judge behavior in terms of intentions and not just outcomes.

Egocentrism

Taking the position of another person is difficult for young children; consequently, their actions often seem one sided or egocentric. This is particularly true for their judgments of the physical world. A four-year-old who may know her right and left hands will have difficulty identifying the right and left hands of a person standing opposite her. To correctly assign right and left to someone standing opposite, we must mentally put ourselves in their physical position; that is something that young children cannot do.

This egocentrism, which is intellectual, should not be identified with a lack of empathy or sympathy (Hoffman, 1977). Young children can identify with the feelings of adults or of other children when these are different from their own, with one proviso: Young children need perceptual clues to the other person's feeling state. A young child, for example, will be able to comfort another child who is crying because the other child's tears are a clear sign of distress. On the other hand, a young child might not be able to understand that an adult who is behaving "normally" is nonetheless quite unhappy.

Language development

In addition to their newly developed abilities to discriminate and group objects according to their qualities (color, form, etc.), young children make a good deal of progress in their language development. By the age of three or four years, many children have an active vocabulary of several thousand words and can construct a variety of sentences (Carey, 1977). Indeed, children of this age often are verbally precocious, and their verbal abilities may far outstrip their cognitive skills. This is one reason that overestimating the intellectual abilities of this age group is easy.

Verbal precocity

A few examples may serve to highlight the discrepancy between young children's verbal precocity and their intellectual understanding. Many young children may have learned to "count" from 1 to 10, yet this may

be rote memorization and has nothing whatever to do with the child's quantitative understanding. If you ask this child to actually count a row of pennies, the child may count the row once as having 8 pennies and another time as having 10 and not experience any sense of conflict. Faced with real objects the child has no awareness of the relation of the terms to the elements and no true understanding of a unit, so although a child may use a unit word, she lacks a true quantitative understanding.

The same is true for many other words used by young children. For example, children of three or four may use the words *dead* or *kill* in appropriate sentences, yet they have no real understanding of life or death in the biological sense. Indeed, young children tend to think of death as going away for a while. A four-year-old, upon returning from his grandfather's funeral where he had witnessed the coffin being lowered into the ground, asked, "When will Grandpa be back?"

Dealing with verbal precocity. Rather than assuming that young children understand words in the same way that adults do, we need to ask them exactly what they mean. Young children are eager and happy to tell adults what they mean using words, and their elaboration is often quite revealing. Listening to children is the key to understanding children on their own terms. If, on the other hand, we assume that they use words with the same comprehension that we do, we attribute undue competence to them.

A similar caution holds for children's questions. Children of three and four years of age are inveterate question askers. More often than not, however, their questions are rhetorical and they have their own answers ready at hand, if only we take the trouble to inquire. A four-year-old once asked me whether traveling by boat or by airplane was better. When I asked him what he thought, he replied, "If you go by water, it is better to go by boat, but if you go by air, it is better to go by plane." It is hard to argue with that very practical logic.

Social development: Acquiring frames

One way of looking at social development is to see it as involving the acquisition of increasingly more complex frames. Erving Goffman (1974) defined frames as the rules, understandings, and expectancies that govern our behavior in repetitive social situations. From an early age, children learn the rules that govern having their diapers changed, being fed, and receiving attention. These rules are implicit and unverbalized, but they regulate the child's behavior nonetheless. Consider the going-to-bed frame that many young children learn once they are ambulatory. They know that before going to bed they must (a) change into their pajamas, (b) brush their teeth, and (c) say goodnight to their parents. Sometimes the frame in-

volves a bedtime story read by the parents. Other frames have to do with eating, visiting relatives, going to the park or playground, and so on. By the time children are three and four years of age, they have a rich repertoire of frames.

Frame rhythms

Frames, in addition to guiding behavior in repetitive social situations, also have emotional rhythms. A good illustration is the story-reading frame. Children like to hear the same story over and over again. They often know the story by heart. If the adult reading the story misses or misreads a word, the child will likely be upset. The frame expectancy, that the story should be read exactly as it has been read before, has been spoiled. Frames have their own emotional rhythms, and when these are not played out, the child is distressed. In frames we see the close connection between the cognitive dimension and the social and emotional facets of development mentioned earlier.

Frame switches

Frames can cause young children emotional distress in other ways, as well, such as during "frame switches." A child may be busy playing with a set of blocks when his mother tells him to put the blocks away because they are going shopping in a few minutes. The child, who may enjoy shopping trips, nonetheless does not stop playing with the blocks. He is in a block-playing frame and has not been adequately prepared to switch frames. Parents would be well advised to give children plenty of advance warning before changing frames. The same advice holds true for teachers of young children.

Frame clashes

A last source of conflict arising from frames has to do with "frame clashes." Many of the frames that children learn in their homes vary from the frames that other children learn in *their* homes or the frames that are set up in a nursery school or preschool class-room. In the classroom, for example, a child must learn to raise her hand before asking a question or making a remark. This class-room frame conflicts with the family frame, in which children can ask questions and make remarks at will. When children are first learning the classroom frames, they may break them, not because of bad manners but because the children are behaving in a frame that clashes with the frame that governs behavior in the classroom. Children can learn place-related frames but may need more time when these frames clash with the frames that they have acquired at home.

Emotional development

Young children tend to be governed by the basic emotions of fear, anger, affection, and happiness. At the same time, they lack a vocabulary for their feelings and tend to express them directly in action. Angry chil-dren lash out at other children or adults. Frightened children huddle close to their par-ents. Happy children show their happiness in their whole demeanor—in their laughter and in the joy of their movements. In the same way, children show their love and affection openly and physically with hugs, strokes, and kisses.

The way in which young children express their emotions is already shaped by the frames they have learned at home. Some families openly express emotions, whereas others do not. Children quickly learn to express their emotions in accord with their family frames. In some families birthday celebrations are joyous affairs, whereas in other families they tend to be rather somber matters. How the child responds emotionally to particular situ-ations will depend, then, on the family in which the child is reared.

In dealing with young children, attending to their particular emotional frames is im-portant. Some young children feel comfort-able with strange adults, move close to them, and like to be touched and patted. Such children usually come from homes wherein the adults are emotionally expressive and

responsive. Other children shy away from strange adults and their reticence needs to be respected. In affective interactions, we should take our cues from the child.

Emotional and behavioral problems

When we deal with the emotional and behavioral problems of young children, we must keep in mind that there is no "sponta-neous combustion," that is, children do not develop problems on their own. Their prob-lems virtually always reflect problems either in the classroom or child care facility or in the home. Even if the child has a physical disability, how she reacts to and deals with that disability is, at least in part, a reflection of how that disability is received in and out of the classroom.

Caregivers working with children of any age must resist the temptation to make the *child* the patient or client. A young child's problems, academic or otherwise, are always a symptom of a larger social problem. If we ignore the larger issue and focus on the child in isolation, we do a disservice to the child and miss the chance to engage in effective remediation. Treating the problem as inher-ent in the child may have more negative effects than would not treating the child at all.

A recent personal experience illustrates this point. I had the opportunity to sit in on an evaluation of a child with special needs in a suburban elementary school. The child had a speech impediment, had been duly tested, and was recommended for a reme-dial program that had been designed for her. Someone mentioned in passing that this girl came to school poorly clothed and without lunch or lunch money. When I asked more about the family situation, I was told that the mother had two children from a former marriage and was living with a man who also had two children. They had one child to-gether. Each of the children had a physical disability. Although the family had financial resources, the mother, who was less than 30 years of age, was overwhelmed.

When I suggested that the girl might be helped if her mother were given some guidance on how to gain assistance from the local social and health care agencies, I was told that what I was suggesting was "social work" and was not part of the evaluator's job, yet the poor care this child was receiving at home clearly contributed to her learning problem. To help children and their families, we sometimes need to step outside our role boundaries and assist the child and the family in any way we can.

Summary and conclusion

Children of three and four years of age are unique. They are at an age of increased intellectual growth, and we must recognize and appreciate the range of variability of that growth when we set up educational programs and assess educational progress. When we deal with young children, we must keep in mind their tendency to think about the world in concrete ways and remember that their language ability often far exceeds their cognitive understanding. The socialization of young children is by means of frames that govern their behavior in repetitive social situations, and adults must understand that children become upset when frames are spoiled, switched, or contradicted. Young children's emotions are simple and are expressed directly in their words and actions.

Children are most like adults in their emotions and least like us in their thoughts. We must, therefore, treat children with the same good manners that we would accord other adults. At the same time, we need to remember that young children may not understand concepts in the same way we do. Put differently, we should treat young children as we might treat a visitor from another country—with good manners but without expecting that they will understand everything we have to say.

References

Bloom, B. (1964). *Stability and change in human characteristics.* New York: Wiley.

Bryant, P. (1972). The understanding of invariance by very young children. *Canadian Journal of Psychology, 26,* 78–96.

Carey, S. (1977). The child as a word learner. In M. Halle, J. Bressman, & G. Miller (Eds.), *Linguistic theory and psychological reality.* Cambridge, MA: M.I.T. Press.

Donaldson, M. (1978). *Children's minds.* New York: Norton.

Elkind, D. (1987). *Miseducation: Preschoolers at risk.* New York: Knopf.

Elkind, D. (1988). *The hurried child.* Reading, MA: Addison-Wesley.

Gelman, R., Meck, E., & Merkin, S. (1986). Young children's numerical competence. *Cognitive Psychology, 16,* 94–143.

Gesell, A., Halverson, H.L., Thompson, H., Ilg, F., Castner, B., Ames, L.B., & Amatruda, C. (1949). *The first five years of life.* New York: Harper.

Goffman, E. (1974). *Frame analysis.* New York: Harper.

Hoffman, M.L. (1977). Empathy: Its developmental and prosocial implications. In C.B. Keasy (Ed.), *Nebraska symposium on motivation.* Lincoln, NE: University of Nebraska Press.

Kamii, C. (Ed.). (1990). *Achievement testing in the early grades.* Washington, DC: NAEYC.

Piaget, J. (1932). *The moral judgment of the child.* New York: Harcourt Brace.

Piaget, J. (1950). *The psychology of intelligence.* London: Routledge & Kegan Paul.

Piaget, J. (1951). *The child's conception of the world.* London: Routledge & Kegan Paul.

Piaget, J. (1952). *The language and thought of the child.* London: Routledge & Kegan Paul.

Tanner, J.M. (1961). *Education and physical growth.* London: University of London Press.

2. Educational Issues and Implications

*I*t has been said of authorship that "of book writing there shall be no end." One might say much the same of educational reform. I was reminded of this when I reread the first essay in this section, "Humanizing the Curriculum." In that essay I suggested that curriculum reform can come about through the three avenues of addition, subtraction, and transformation, and I gave examples of all three types of reform. Although the topics are different today than they were more than a decade ago, we are still following the same three avenues of reform.

Today there is as much pressure to add "multicultural" material to the curriculum as there was to "humanize" the curriculum in the 1970s. The issue of the developmental appropriateness of these additions is as relevant to the multicultural curriculum as it was to the humanistic curriculum. Likewise, in these times of tight budgets and concerns about our children's poor educational performance vis-à-vis that of children in other countries, the arts again are the first to be subtracted from the curriculum. Other valuable activities are being subtracted as well, such as playground time and recess. The idea that if children are not doing well academically the problem is that they are not working diligently enough dies very hard indeed.

Although the topics to be added and subtracted from the curriculum are different today, the goal of effective transformation remains the same. We still need to find ways to keep our schools up-to-date in terms of knowledge and technology, and this learning must be in keeping with individual and age differences in children's interests and abilities. This goal will only be realized when subject matter experts work cooperatively and respectfully with teachers and child development specialists.

In rereading "We Can Teach Reading Better," I again had the reaction that in education things are "always changing, always the same." We have much more research on reading today than we did when that piece was written. There is considerable evidence that the whole language approach to reading, which sees reading as but one facet of language, is an effective way to contextualize learning to read. Reading to children and having children relate and write their own stories without concern for accuracy (invented spellings) are all parts of the learning-to-read *process. I am pleased to see that I included much of this whole language approach in my essay nearly two decages ago. I still believe in the value of the research reported in the article and its relevance for reading instruction. To my mind, educators and researchers still do not pay enough attention to the relation of cognitive development to reading, despite the fact that all the evidence continues to point in that direction. I should say, however, that although my research and the thrust of my argument were focused upon visual perception, recent research has highlighted the importance of auditory perception. Auditory discrimination appears to be a critical component of successful early reading.*

This finding has an important practical implication for early childhood education. Young children should probably not watch more than an hour or two of television each day. In watching television children can avoid listening and get most of the information visually. Developing this tendency can impair their reading progress quite independently of their level of cognitive development.

*In many ways, the arguments in the essay "Resistance to Developmentally Appropriate Practice: A Case Study of Educational Inertia" are a distillation of arguments I have been making in many different ways over the years. Piaget was fond of saying that "every psychology presupposes an epistemology," that is, a set of assumptions about the process of knowing. He argued that until psychologists appreciated the epistemology under which they were operating, they would make only limited progress. Much the same can be said for education. **Every system of education presupposes an educational philosophy.** Only when we appreciate these philosophical underpinnings can we go beyond them. That, in essence, is the thesis of this essay.*

Humanizing the Curriculum

Educational programs, of whatever kind, must meet two basic yet contradictory human needs. One is the need for *individuality*–the striving to be unique and to realize one's full powers and potentials. The other need is for human *sociality*–the need to relate to other people and to subordinate one's personal inclinations for the benefit of others. In a broad sense, any educational program meeting one or both of these basic human needs could be said to be "humanistic." But in a narrower sense, humanistic education might be limited to those programs providing equal opportunity for learners to realize their individuality *and* their sociality. In this essay I discuss humanizing the curriculum in the broad sense and outline three contemporary approaches to curriculum reform. We can distinguish these approaches by their tendency to *add to*, *substract from*, or *transform* existing curricula.

Adding to the curriculum

When an existing curriculum does not allow sufficient opportunity for human individuality, new curricula may be added to the old. In recent years, for example, a variety of so-called *affective* curricula have been proposed and have been added to the school program at different levels. Schools have implemented innovations such as classroom meetings, values clarification, and moral discussions to help children understand themselves and others better. Many of these activities are indeed useful to teachers and to children. They provide an additional set of tools and procedures to be used in educational practice and thus enrich the teachers' armamentarium.

But the affective curricula can present problems, as well. They can, and often do, perpetuate the same errors that are embedded in traditional school curricula. Many aspects of the school curricula are too difficult for the cognitive level of the children to whom they are directed. Social studies offers a case in point. As this course is commonly pursued, teaching first grade children about the different cultures of the world may be a futile exercise. How can one expect young children, who cannot fully comprehend the ethnic differences in their own community, to understand the world of Australian aborigines?

Many of the affective curricula used in schools repeat the error of demanding tasks beyond children's level of cognitive ability. Many children of elementary school age, for example, are not able to rank their feelings from 1 to 5, nor are they always able to reflect upon their own thinking in ways that permit assigning clear priorities to what they want most or least (my 11-year-old son has changed his mind five times about what he wants for his upcoming birthday). Children's priorities are shifting and transient rather than abiding or lasting. Is it worthwhile to put children through the procedure of assigning priorities that are momentary at best?

Moreover, if the affective curricula are added to the school curricula, they can become a burden to teachers, who already have so much to "cover" and so little time in which to do so that imposing additional curricula may hinder rather than help them. Moreover, some affective curricula can backfire. A child whose parent has just died or a child whose parents have just been divorced may be deeply embarrassed or hurt by being required to reveal publicly feelings that are legitimately personal. Affective curricula that involve procedures geared to the child's level of understanding and meshed with the school curriculum can be beneficial, but if these methods and procedures are foisted upon the teacher as additional educational "objectives," the result may be just the opposite of what was intended.

Subtracting from the curriculum

A somewhat different approach to curriculum reform is taken when current educational practices are regarded as not sufficiently geared to socialization—to the acquisition of skills required for the individual's successful adaptation to society. The back-to-basics movement has reflected this approach. It argues that too much attention in education has been paid to individuality and too little to sociality. Accordingly, people who advocate back-to-basics often want to subtract those aspects of the educational program that speak to human individuality, namely, the arts. Presumably, the less time spent on the arts, the more time available to spend on the fundamentals.

In my opinion the back-to-basics movement, like that of affective education, is based on a false premise. Affective education may lead to the inference that cognitive and affective processes are distinct and have to be addressed separately. Good teaching, however, is af-

fective *and* cognitive, and the successful teacher is always "half ham and half egghead." Teachers' enthusiasm for the subject matter and their respect and good feeling for children provide all the affective education a child needs in the school setting.

The back-to-basics movement is based on another false premise of a different order than the one that gave rise to affective education, namely, that if children today are doing worse in academic subjects than they were a decade ago, their poor performance *must* be due to our having been too soft and too permissive. The widely reported drop in SAT scores over the past 15 years has often been interpreted in this way. Critics have argued that the drop was caused by schools' not requiring children to read and write enough and by young people's wasting time watching television.

The belief that decline in performance must be a result of sloth is, of course, deeply embedded in our Puritan heritage, but in this case it happens to be wrong. Just about 15 years ago, the "new" curricula hit the schools—stimulated by the pressure Americans felt from the successful launching of Sputnik by the USSR. These curricula, created by university professors, were up-to-date—with the "new math" and "psycholinguistic" reading programs, not to mention a plethora of science programs. These curricula were much more hard nosed than the child-centered "progressive" materials that preceded them. Far from being "soft" on children, the new curricula were more difficult than many others in recent American educational history. One could argue that the drop in SAT scores reflected the fact that the new curricula were too *hard* rather than too easy.

Some evidence favors this argument; for example, although SAT scores in math and reading went down, scores in creativity and analytic skills went up—just what one would expect if the new curricula were very challenging. In dealing with curricula that stretch or exceed the limits of their comprehension, children have to be both analytical (to figure

out what is going on) and creative (to find their own ways to deal with the curriculum demands). In addition, some of the curriculum materials now coming out reflect that the back-to-basics curricula are easier and more child-centered than much of the curricula of the '60s!

The back-to-basics movement, then, although starting from a false premise, has had some positive effects. Under the guise of "getting tougher" on children, the new curricula have in fact often gotten easier, and this change may be all to the good. Some recent data from the National Assessment of Academic Achievement indicate that reading scores for 9-year-olds have gone up over the past four years but that this finding does not also apply to 13- or 17-year-olds. My interpretation of these findings is that these nine-year-old children are products of the new curricula, which are child-centered and concrete.

The negative aspect of the back-to-basics movement in elementary education is the de-emphasis of the arts. If the back-to-basics movement's aim is to enhance children's social adaptation, then de-emphasizing the arts is a sad mistake. The arts are social as well as individual. In a very real sense, the arts are a basic means of social communication and a way that individuals can share a sense of beauty. By de-emphasizing the arts the back-to-basics movement deprives children of a prime means for reconciling the conflicting demands of sociality and individuality.

Transforming the curriculum

When the curriculum does not pay sufficient heed to the integration of individuality and sociality, a different approach to curriculum reform is taken. People who see the curriculum in this way want to neither add to nor subtract from the existing curriculum but rather to *transform* it in such a way that the needs for individuality and sociality can be brought into harmony. To my mind, this approach to education is best exemplified by the informal or "open-education" movement.

In many ways the open-education movement is a modern version of Dewey's "project" method, in which both social adaptation and child interest were taken into account in choosing curriculum materials.

The open-education approach to curriculum is too well known to be reviewed in detail here. Such programs allow for child choice and allow children to take responsibility for their own learning. The programs emphasize teacher-made rather than commercial materials, and the teaching is heavily experience based. The school day is loosely organized into large blocks of time rather than into closely clocked intervals. Open education accords great emphasis to the arts as an integral part of education, particularly in providing means of expression. In all of these ways, open education tries to transform the curriculum so that the needs for individuality and sociality reinforce and complement, rather than conflict with, one another.

The open-education approach to curriculum is not without its problems, however.* Good informal education is hard work. The teacher constantly has to fight the temptation to institutionalize innovation, and nothing is more deadly to children's interest than an overdone idea. We must face the opposite danger as well. I have seen children engaged in truly innovative science or math activities

that were both interesting and fun, but these activities were not integrated with the rest of the school program, and neither I nor the children could see where the activities were leading. In the same way, I have seen children so conditioned to asking questions that they no longer bother to wait for the answers. Done well, open education can be a model of truly humanistic education; done poorly, it can be a disaster.

Conclusion

In this essay I have briefly outlined three contemporary approaches to humanizing the curriculum, to reconciling each person's need for individuality and sociality. Each of the approaches—affective education, back-to-basics education, and open education—speaks to an important need or needs. Each approach has limitations as well as virtues. We find, then, no one single answer to humanizing the curriculum. How we approach the task will depend upon our world view and our priorities regarding human individuality and sociality. Children can adapt to and profit from each of these approaches as long as we take any approach with the children in mind. In the broadest sense, humanizing the curriculum means putting child need and child ability into the curriculum equation.

---

* The "open-education" approach of the '60s and '70s for the most part was not well implemented in the United States. Teachers too often were not involved in the decision to move to the open-education approach, and they did not receive the necessary training and pedagogical approach. Moreover, in some instances, open education was interpreted to mean that teachers should completely abdicate their role. Such problems and excesses notwithstanding, many themes of open education were valid and echoed Dewey's ideas about progressive education. Many of these themes may also be found in statements of developmentally appropriate practice (Bredekamp, 1987; Bredekamp & Rosegrant, 1992), which have attempted to clarify aspects, such as the teacher's role, to avoid past misinterpretations.

References

Bredekamp, S. (Ed.). (1987). *Developmentally appropriate practice in early childhood programs serving children from birth through age 8* (rev. ed.). Washington, DC: NAEYC.
Bredekamp, S., & Rosegrant, T. (Eds.). (1992). *Reaching potentials: Appropriate curriculum and assessment for young children: Volume 1.* Washington, DC: NAEYC.

We Can Teach Reading Better

C an we do a better job of teaching children to read? Yes, I believe we can if we take into consideration how their minds develop. To illustrate this point I will discuss beginning reading and the child's conception of letters and then move on to how children who are more advanced readers use their accumulated storehouse of knowledge to give meaning to the printed word.

The early stages of learning to read

A basic error in much beginning reading instruction centers on the concept of the letter, which is, in many ways, the basic unit of reading. To the adult, the letter appears as a discrete object that is a conventional representation of one or more sounds, but the letter as adults see it is not the letter known to the beginning reader.

As Piaget points out, children and adults see the world in different ways. The well-known "conservation" experiments are a case in point. Most adults are amazed to discover that young children believe that changing the shape of a piece of clay will change the *amount* of clay. This amazement suggests that most adults assume that children see the world in much the same way they do. Adults make this assumption because they are unable to recall or reconstruct the course of their own cognitive growth.

This phenomenon, the loss of awareness of their part in the construction of reality, is what Piaget means by *externalization.*

Externalization serves a useful adaptive purpose and allows the individual to operate more effectively in the environment. Externalization only becomes a problem when we try to teach the young, that is, when we try to present material that we have already mastered. We as adults, who have conceptualized and externalized many facets of the world, have trouble appreciating the difficulties children encounter in their attempts to make sense out of their world.

From the child's point of view, the concept of the letter poses many of the same problems as do concepts of number, space, and time. Before the age of six or seven, most children lack a true conception of unit or number because they cannot coordinate two dimensions or relationships simultaneously. Such coordinations are basic to the construction of a unit concept because a unit is, by definition, both like every other unit and different from every other unit in its order or enumeration.

In many ways children's problems in understanding the concept of a letter are even more difficult than the problems they encounter in constructing the concept of a number. Like numbers, letters have an ordinal property, which is their position in the alphabet. Letters also have a cardinal property, which is their name (*A, B, C,* etc.) and which each letter shares with all other letters of the same name (all *B*'s are *B*, and so on).

Letters are even more complicated than are numbers because, in addition to letters' ordinal and cardinal properties, they have phonic contextual properties. One letter can stand for one or more sounds, and one sound can be represented by different letters; hence, to have a full understanding of phonics, a child may need to have some of the logical abilities that are not acquired by most children until around the age of six or seven.

Many different kinds of evidence support this logical analysis of the difficulties in early reading. Written languages that are more regularly phonetic than is English are apparently much easier to learn to read. In these alphabets, such as Japanese, difficulties with logical operations do not exist because one and the same element always has one and the same sound regardless of its position or phonetic context.

Reading achievement and logical ability have been found to be highly correlated; average readers are superior in logical ability to slow readers of comparable overall intelligence. Moreover, training children in logical skills has a significant positive effect upon some aspects of reading achievement.

These findings are consistent with the view that some of the understandings underlying the concept of a letter require logical abilities that are not fully elaborated, according to Piaget, until the stage of *concrete operations* at about age six or seven. To test this hypothesis in still another way, a collaborator and I have begun, in the last few years, to look at the cognitive competencies of children who learn to read early, that is, children who can read before they enter kindergarten. One of our hypotheses was that if reading involves concrete operations, which are usually attained at age six to seven, then early readers should show these abilities at an early age. In addition to assessing children's cognitive abilities, we were also interested in the personal/social characteristics of these children and in the educational/emotional climate that prevails in their homes.

We have now completed two studies of early readers, one with 16 early readers and another with 38. In both studies we matched the children who could read upon kindergarten entry with a control group of children who could not read upon kindergarten entry on such things as age, sex, IQ, and socioeconomic status. All of the children were given a large battery of achievement and intelligence tests as well as personality and creativity tests. We also interviewed their parents. In both studies we found that children who could read upon kindergarten entry did better on Piagetian measures of conservation than did those who could not read upon kindergarten entry. They also performed better on certain psycholinguistic measures, such as sound blending.

I must emphasize, however, that cognitive construction of a letter is only one of the requirements for successful reading. Our parent-interview data suggest that a rich background of early experience with spoken and written language provided in homes where books and magazines are plentiful and where parents frequently read to the children is also important for successful reading. In addition, social motivation to please significant adults appears to be a necessary, if not sufficient, factor in giving zest even to the mechanical aspects of learning to read.

In considering cognitive development and early reading, we must therefore avoid the two extremes that are sometimes advocated when cognitive "readiness" is discussed. One extreme is the effort to train children of preschool age in cognitive abilities that they have not yet attained; I have seen no evidence that such early intervention has any lasting effectiveness. The alternative extreme, allowing children to learn in their own time and in their own way, is also unwarranted. Children need to be taught to read but only after they have demonstrated the requisite cognitive abilities.

In summary, I can identify at least four requirements for successful beginning reading: a language-rich environment, attachment to adults who model and reward reading behavior, attainment of concrete operations, and an instructional program. All other things being equal—namely, that the children are of at least average intellectual ability and are free of serious emotional or physical disabilities—the presence of these four characteristics should ensure that most children will learn to read with reasonable ease and considerable enjoyment.

Advanced reading and comprehension

Let us now turn to advanced reading and the construction of meaning. I have already suggested that the intellectual processes involved in beginning reading are analogous to those involved in concept formulation. A child who is learning to read has to coordinate similarities and differences and construct concepts of letters that are both *like* every other letter in that they represent sounds but *different* in the specific sounds that they represent.

Concept formation involves inferential processes, and these can be observed in beginning reading as well. Many errors in beginning reading, such as reading *where* for *when*, are inferential errors rather than discrimination errors. The child is inferring the whole from observing the part (the *wh*). Such inferential errors are high-level cognitive errors inasmuch as the child is erring in a way that more advanced and accomplished readers do. We should encourage these processes by temporarily sacrificing accuracy for fluency. Experience indicates that once children are fluent readers, they can correct for accuracy, but overconcern with accuracy can retard fluent reading.

When concept formation and inferential aspects of reading have become automatic and children can recognize printed words quickly and easily, they enter the phase of rapid silent reading. In silent reading the major cognitive task is no longer concept formation and inference but rather interpretation, the construction of meaning. In constructing meanings, children have to relate representations—in this case, printed words—to their own concepts and ideas. Success in interpretation, or comprehension, depends upon a different set of characteristics than does learning to read: visual

advanced readers. Apparently, motoric identification and discrimination of letters, as advocated by Montessori, are beneficial in the beginning phases of learning to read, but the coordination of visual and motor processes has to be given up if more rapid reading is to develop.

Put more concretely, beginning readers use their fingers as markers to help direct their attention and exploration of printed matter, but once they become advanced readers, using a finger as a marker would impede reading. Rapid reading requires independence from the tactile motor system.

Some of my recent work on perceptual exploration and memory demonstrates this growth of visual independence in another way. Children at different age levels (age four through eight) were shown large cards upon which were pasted 16 pictures of familiar objects. On one card the pictures were pasted in an upright position, whereas on another the same pictures were pasted upside down. At each age level, half of the children viewed the cards with the pictures upright, while the other half viewed the cards with the upside-down pictures. Each child had two tasks: to name each of the objects on the cards and then to recall as many of the objects as possible once the cards were turned over.

Young children (age four to five) displayed a significant difference in recall scores in favor of the upside-down pictures. This difference, however, diminishes as children grow older and disappears at about age eight or nine. Children with limited hearing, who use finger spelling and vocalization in communication, also show a tendency to recall the upside-down pictures more accurately. This finding suggests that in young children the motoric system is still tied to the visual system. In identifying the upside-down pictures, these children may implicitly try to

independence, meaning construction, and receptive discipline.

Visual independence

Rapid silent reading and comprehension require, at the outset, that the visual verbal system become independent of the sensory motor system. Rapid reading involves fewer motor fixations and wider visual segments of scanning, and this in turn means less motor involvement and more conceptual inferential activity. In effect, in rapid silent reading the brain does more work and the eyes do less. Recent evidence supports the importance of visual independence in advanced reading. Although tactile discrimination of sandpaper letters is positively correlated with reading achievement among beginning readers, we find it is negatively correlated with reading achievement among

"right" the figures, thereby increasing motoric involvement. It seems reasonable to assume that the increased motoric involvement and attendant heightened attention account for young children's superior memory for upside-down pictures. Among older children, in whom identification can occur without implicit motoric "righting," this attentional advantage with upside-down pictures is no longer present. Direct as well as indirect evidence thus indicates that rapid, silent reading requires considerable visual independence from the tactile motor system.

Meaning construction

A second prerequisite to advanced silent reading is facility in meaning construction. From a cognitive-development point of view, reading comprehension is not a passive process of decoding written symbols; on the contrary, it is a constructive activity analogous to creative writing.

Meaning is not inherent in written or spoken words; rather, words are given meaning by readers or listeners who interpret them within their own storehouse of knowledge. Silent readers give meaning to the words they read by relating these words to the conceptual system they have constructed in the course of their development. The richness of meaning they derive from their reading depends upon the quality of the material and the breadth and depth of the readers' conceptual understanding. Readers often derive satisfaction in reading, at least in part, from the degree of fit between the material being read and their own conceptual level.

A recent doctoral dissertation supports this position (Schlager, 1974). The author chose 33 books that had won the prestigious Newbery Medal awards of excellence. She then determined how frequently each book had been checked out of a number of libraries over the preceding three-year period. Taking the five most frequently chosen and the five least frequently chosen books, she then analyzed them from the standpoint of their congruence with the conceptual ability of the age group for which they were written. She found that the five most frequently chosen books were congruent with the cognitive level of the children for whom they were written, while this was not true of the five least frequently chosen books. Apparently, other things being equal, children prefer stories that have meaning within their own cognitive organization.

Comprehension, or construction of meanings, is also helped by children's efforts to give meaning to, that is, to represent their own experiences. The more opportunity children have to experience the effort and satisfaction of representing their own thoughts verbally and otherwise, the better prepared they will be to interpret the representations of others.

Teachers today often do not leave time for children to write, creatively or otherwise, but I believe that the more children write, the more they will get from their reading. Writing and reading are reciprocal processes of meaning construction that mutually reinforce one another.

Receptive discipline

A third prerequisite to effective silent reading seems at first to be a contradiction to what has just been said about the readers being active participants in the process: The reader must have a receptive attitude, a willingness to respond to the representations of others. Good readers, like good listeners, have to be simultaneously passive (receptive to the representations of others) and active (interpreting those representations within their own conceptual framework).

Many young people are poor readers for the same reason that they are poor listeners: They are more interested in representing their own thoughts and ideas than they are in interpreting the thoughts and ideas of others. They lack what might be called *receptive discipline*. Young people demonstrate receptive discipline when they attend fully to the representations of others and resist following their own free associations and tangents. Many so-called slow readers have problems with receptive discipline and not with rapid reading.

Receptive discipline is not innate; it can be facilitated and taught. Text material that is of interest to readers and is at their level of competence facilitates a receptive attitude. Another way to encourage receptive discipline is to have goals for nonrecreational reading. When young people (or adults, for that matter) know that they will have to present what they have read to a group, they are likely to be more attentive than they would be if they had no such goal.

*   *   *

These are but a few examples of techniques that might be employed to encourage receptive discipline. Whatever techniques are used, receptive discipline seems to be an important ingredient for successful reading comprehension.

Conclusion

I have pointed out some of the ways in which reading, from the earliest through the more advanced stages, involves active, conceptual processes. Understanding better what is involved in learning to read and in being a proficient reader is the first step in improving the teaching of reading.

Reference

Schlager, N. (1974). *Developmental factors influencing children's responses to literature.* Unpublished doctoral dissertation, Claremont College of Education, Claremont, CA.

The original version of this essay appeared in *Today's Education,* (1975), *64*(4), 34–38. Used with permission.

Resistance to Developmentally Appropriate Practice: A Case Study of Educational Inertia

American education is heavily institutionalized. It is closely tied to colleges and universities that engage in teacher training and to various research-oriented graduate schools of education. Education in this country has equally strong ties to the multibillion-dollar educational publishing industry. In addition, education is dependent upon local, state, and federal government for funding. In the past few decades, the federal government has become much more involved in education by funding various titled programs for children who are disadvantaged and disabled. Moreover, in many communities local school boards dictate educational policy with little or no educational expertise to back them up. Finally, educational systems, particularly in large cities, are heavily bureaucratized.

Because education is so closely intermeshed with other social institutions, true educational reform can only come about when a systemic change simultaneously alters all of the intertwined components of the educational establishment. Such a systemic change, however, has to begin at the philosophical and conceptual level because all of the various components of the educational system share an implicit educational philosophy. This philosophy, which might be called *psychometric,* views education from a quantitative perspective that I will describe in more detail in this essay. This shared underlying philosophy welds the various components of the educational system together and is the true barrier to authentic educational reform.

This philosophical and conceptual barrier is the real reason that contemporary classroom innovations and curricular reforms have little or no chance of effecting any significant, lasting change in education. If the educational innovation is in keeping with the underlying philosophy, then it is not truly innovative and will change nothing. On the other hand, if the innovation is at variance with the underlying philosophy, it will never be properly implemented and will eventually be rejected as unworkable.

A current example of an educational innovation at variance with the underlying educational philosophy is the concept of "developmentally appropriate practice." A comparison of the philosophy underlying this conception and the philosophy that dictates extant educational practice makes me pessimistic about the chances of developmentally appropriate practice being widely implemented in our schools. The comparison thus provides an interesting case study of how underlying philosophies can determine the acceptance or rejection of a particular educational innovation.

The principle of developmentally appropriate educational practice, that the curriculum should be matched to the child's level of developmental ability (Bredekamp, 1987), has been favorably received in educational circles. This positive reception is, on the face of it, quite extraordinary. In fact, developmentally appropriate practice represents a philosophy of education in total opposition to the "psychometric" educational philosophy that dictates educational practice in the majority of our public schools. Perhaps that is why developmental appropriateness has been honored more in word than in deed.

My first aim in this essay is to highlight some of the differences between these two educational philosophies. My second aim is to contrast a few of the practical educational implications of the two philosophies. Finally, I will argue that true educational reform in this country will only come about when we have a paradigm shift away from the reigning psychometric educational psychology.

Two philosophies of education

Any philosophy of education must include a conception of the learner, the learning process, the information to be acquired, and the goals or aims of education. The developmental philosophy differs from the psychometric philosophy on all four counts. The developmental approach presented here derives from the research and theory of Jean Piaget (1950).

The conception of the learner

Within a developmental philosophy of education, the learner is viewed as having *developing* mental abilities. All individuals except for those with severe mental disabilities are assumed to attain these abilities, although all individuals may not all attain them at the same pace. We expect, for example, that all children will attain the concrete operations that Piaget described as emerging at about the age of six or seven (Piaget, 1950). These operations, which function much like the group arithmetic operations, enable children who have attained them to learn rules and to apply them. Not all children will attain these operations at the same age. Individual differences in ability thus reflect differences in rates of intellectual growth.

This conception of mental ability contrasts with that of a psychometric philosophy of education, which views the learner as having *measurable* abilities. The psychometric position assumes that any ability that exists must exist in some amount and is therefore quantifiable. For example, intelligence tests—the flagship of the psychometric philosophy—are designed to assess individual differences in the ability to learn and to adapt to new situations. From the psychometric perspective, individual differences in performance reflect differences in *amount* of ability.

These opposed conceptions of human ability, both of which contain some truth, have far different pedagogical implications. From a developmental perspective, which views abilities as growing, the important task is to *match curricula* to the level of children's emerging mental abilities—hence the principle of developmental appropriateness. Curricular materials should only be introduced when the child has attained the level of mental ability needed to master those materials. This in turn means that curricula have to be studied and analyzed to determine the level of mental ability required to comprehend them.

A case in point is the concept of number. Piaget's work demonstrates clearly that children acquire the concept of number in a sequence of stages that are related to age (Piaget, 1952). At the first stage (age three to four), the young child has a concept of nominal number, in which number is equivalent to the numerals on a basketball or football jersey. At the second stage (age four to five), the child arrives at an understanding of ordinal number and grasps that one number means more than another, but not by how much. Number is a rank without units. Only by the age of six or seven do children attain a true, or unit, conception of number, wherein a number stands for a fixed unit or number of units. The practical implications of the development of number understanding have been well described by Constance Kamii (1982).

From a psychometric point of view, however, the most important thing is to *match children* of equal amounts of ability. Bright children are assumed to be able to learn more per unit of time than are less intelligent children. In practice this results in so-called ability grouping, which in effect allows bright children to go through material more quickly than slower children. This psychometric orientation also underlies the provision of special classes for children at both the high and low end of the intellectual spectrum. These are critical issues that warrant much more detailed treatment than can be given here. From a developmental point of view, however, in the majority of cases, ability grouping is a strategy for avoiding developmentally appropriate practice.

The conception of the learning process

Within the developmental philosophy of education, learning is a *creative* activity. Whenever we learn we engage the world in such a way as to create something new that reflects both our own mental activity and the material with which we have engaged. We do not simply copy content but stamp it with our own unique way of viewing the world. The child from Connecticut who heard the Lord's Prayer as "Our Father in art in New Haven, Harold be they name" is not the exception but the rule. Everything we learn has a subjective as well as an objective component.

The conception of learning as a creative or constructive process has a very important practical implication: we cannot consider learning independently of the content to be learned. The material to be learned interacts with the learning process in some special way. Long after Piaget discovered the successive stages and organizations of mental operations, he continued to study how children attained different concepts, such as space, geometry, time, and movement and speed (Piaget & Inhelder, 1956; Piaget, Inhelder, & Szeminska, 1960; Piaget, 1967, 1970). In so doing he emphasized that knowing the stages of mental development does not provide any special insight into how children use these operations in attaining a concept. The only way to discover how children go about learning specific subject matter is to study how they use their mental abilities to master the material.

From the psychometric point of view, in contrast, learning consists of a set of principles (such as intermittent reinforcement) or a set of skills (such as decoding), which are independent of the content to be learned. Early workers in this tradition enunciated principles such as "mass" versus "distributed" or "whole" versus "part" learning, which

lems, they employ complex problem-solving activities, namely, *strategies.* Put differently, the content of the problem determines the level of problem-solving activities that people employ.

This insight seems to have been lost. The current interest in teaching children thinking skills (Baron & Sternberg, 1987), learning strategies (Weinstein & Mayer, 1986), or computer programming (Papert, 1980) is a regression to the idea that thought and content can be treated separately. Proponents of this philosophy assume that once children learn thinking skills or learning strategies, these skills will automatically be transferred to new content. Transfer of training does occur, of course, but it is far from automatic. Transfer works when children are active, not passive, learners (Perkins & Salomon, 1988), but what does activity mean if not that the child is aware of the contents about which she is thinking or to which she is applying strategies. Mental process is always content oriented.

The developmental approach recognizes that transfer of skills or understandings from one subject to another is limited and rarely automatic. This lack of transfer is not because there are no general abilities but rather because each subject is different and requires a *novel utilization* of general strategies for dealing with its realm of subject matter. Writers learn general strategies for dealing with plots, characters, and so on, and researchers learn general strategies for dealing with their chosen matters of investigation. These general strategies are nonetheless limited to a particular realm of problems and usually do not work when one ventures far outside that realm.

In contrast, the psychometric approach assumes automatic transfer of learned strategies and skills across subject-matter areas because it assumes that the common ele-

presumably operate independently of the content to be learned. Early studies of memory employed nonsense syllables specifically to eliminate the effect of content on the study of the memory process (Murray, 1980).

The limitations of this attempt to divorce content from process were dramatically demonstrated by Bruner, Goodnow, and Austin in their seminal work on problem solving (1956). Until this publication, problem solving had been discussed in terms of "trial and error" (Thorndike, 1921) or sudden "insight" (Kohler, 1927; Duncker, 1945), and much of the work on problem solving was done with animals. What Bruner and his colleagues demonstrated was that when you present human subjects with complex prob-

ments that all subjects share are more salient than their individual variations.

This difference between the developmental and psychometric approaches contains a certain irony. The developmental approach is generally regarded as a *nature* approach because of its emphasis on development; the stages and the limits are set by growth and maturation. The psychometric approach, on the other hand, is regarded as a *nurture* approach because of its heavy emphasis on environmental influences. Yet when it comes to transfer, it is the developmental approach that places emphasis on the uniqueness of content (the environment), while the psychometric approach dismisses environmental variability and emphasizes the generalizability of mental processes.

The concept of knowledge

From a developmental perspective, then, knowledge is always a construction, and the result is inevitably a joint product representing contributions of the subject and the object. This idea is far from new; it harks back to the Kantian resolution of idealist (all knowledge is a mental construction) and the empiricist (all knowledge is a copy of an externally existing world) interpretations of how we come to know the world (Kant, 1943). Kant argues that the mind provides the "categories" of knowing, while the real world provides the content. Knowledge is thus a construction of the mind interacting with the world and cannot be reduced to either one.

What Piaget added to the Kantian solution—and what makes Piaget a neo-Kantian—was his demonstration that the categories of knowing (the mental operations of intelligence) are not constant, as Kant supposed; rather, they change with age (Piaget, 1972). This adds a developmental dimension to the Kantian version of the construction of knowledge. As their mental operations develop, children are required to reconstruct the realities they elaborated at the previous developmental level. In effect, the child creates reality, and recreates it, out of her or his experiences with the environment.

The reality of the young child, his knowledge of the world, is thus different than the reality of the older child and of the adult. Young children, for example, believe that a quantity changes in amount when it changes in appearance—say, that the amount of liquid in a low, flat container increases when the liquid is poured into a tall, narrow container. Older children have a different reality and appreciate the fact that a quantity remains the same despite any change in appearance—that quantity is conserved. Looked at in this way, the young child's conception of quantity is not "wrong" but is, in fact, as developmentally appropriate as is the older child's grasp of conservation.

From the psychometric point of view, on the other hand, knowledge is something that the subject acquires and that can be measured independently from the processes of acquisition. This separation is reflected in the distinction between intelligence (ability) and achievement (content) tests. One consequence of the separation between learning and content is that knowledge can be measured against an external standard and independent of the learner. When compared to this external standard, the child's responses can be assessed as either right or wrong.

In some types of knowledge there are right and wrong answers. The Bastille was stormed in 1789, not 1650, and two plus two equals four, not five. We have to distinguish between what I have called *fundamental* knowledge (Elkind, 1987), which we construct on our own, and *derived* knowledge, which is constructed by others and which we acquire secondhand. The terms *right* and *wrong* are useful in connection with derived knowledge but not with fundamental knowledge. We must recognize, however, that even derived knowledge has a subjective component. Derived knowledge is always encrusted with personal associations. We may remember dates by associating them with particular images, math facts with the aid of rhymes, and so on.

The developmental approach introduces the idea that differences in knowledge can exist without these differences being right or wrong. The idea of difference, rather than right or wrong, is important not only with respect to fundamental knowledge but also with respect to creative thinking. Many bright children, for example, come up with ideas that are different from those of their peers or teachers, but these ideas are often treated as wrong rather than as different and original. One bright child, when asked to write something about the color blue, talked about Picasso's blue period and was teased and jeered at by the other children. A greater respect for appreciating differences as well as right or wrong would reduce the stress that so many bright children experience in our schools.

Teaching children that some knowledge, qualities, and traits are neither right nor wrong, just different, is important from many perspectives. A nonjudgmental approach to social traits, for example, is essential in teaching children about different cultures, religions, and languages. Being nonjudgmental is also useful in teaching children about the arts. Young people need to learn that different people can have contrasting tastes in music, literature, and art and that these tastes are not right or wrong, simply different.

The aims of education

Given this description of the developmental philosophy of education, the aims of developmental education are straightforward. If the learner is seen as a growing individual with developing abilities, if learning is regarded as a creative activity, and if knowledge is seen as a construction, then the aim of education must surely be to facilitate this growth, this creative activity, and this construction of knowledge. Piaget described the aims of education from a developmental perspective this way:

The principal goal of education is to create men who are capable of doing new things, not simply repeating what other generations have done—

men who are creative, inventive, and discoverers. The second goal of education is to form minds which can be critical, can verify, and not accept everything that is offered. The great danger today is of slogans, collective opinions, ready made trends of thought. We have to be able to resist them individually, to criticize, to distinguish between what is proven and what is not. So we need pupils who are active, who learn early to find out by themselves, partly by their own spontaneous activity and partly through material we set up for them; who learn early to tell what is verifiable and what is simply the first idea to come to them. (Ripple & Rockcastle, 1964)

The aim of developmental education, then, is to produce creative, critical thinkers. This aim is not achieved by teaching children and adolescents thinking skills but rather by creating developmentally appropriate learning environments that will encourage and challenge the child's emerging mental abilities. Creative and critical thinking are not skills to be taught and learned but rather basic orientations toward self and the world that can only be acquired when children are actively engaged in constructing and reconstructing their physical, social, and moral worlds.

In contrast, the aims of psychometric education are to produce children who will score high on tests of achievement—in other words, to maximize the acquisition of quantifiable knowledge and skills. Perhaps former Secretary of Education William J. Bennett expressed this view of the aims of education as well as anyone:

We should want every student to know how mountains are made, and that for most reactions there is an equal and opposite reaction. They should know who said "I am the state" and who said "I have a dream." They should know about subjects and predicates, about isosceles triangles and ellipses. They should know where the Amazon flows and what the First Amendment means. They should know about the Donner party and about slavery, and Shylock, Hercules, and Abigail Adams, where Ethiopia is, and why there is a Berlin Wall. (Bennett, 1986, p. 3)

In this statement Bennett echoes a theme that was also sounded in the influential monograph *A Nation at Risk*, which was published three years earlier and which decried the poor performance of American children on achievement tests compared to the performance of children from other countries, particularly Japan (National Commission on Excellence in Education, 1983). Bennett's remarks also foreshadowed the best-selling critiques of education by Bloom (1987) and Hirsch (1987), who also see American education as failing to educate children with the basic knowledge of Western civilization.

To be sure, young people should be exposed to Shakespeare, know the basics of geography, and be familiar with current events; a developmental approach does not deny the value and importance of such knowledge. The question is what comes first. From a developmental perspective, children who are curious, active learners will acquire much of the knowledge that writers like Bennett, Bloom, and Hirsch advocate—and many other things as well. But creating curious, active learners *has to precede* the acquisition of particular information, and therein lies the difference between the two philosophies of education. To put the difference more succinctly, the developmental approach tries to create children who *want to know,* whereas the psychometric approach seeks to produce children who *know what we want them to know.*

Practical implications of the developmental philosophy

Now that we have looked at these two contrasting educational philosophies, we can review a few of the implications of a developmental perspective for the practice of education. Again, my interpretation is largely based on the Piagetian conception of the development of intelligence.

Teacher training: The teacher as a child development specialist

In most disciplines, students have to learn the basic material of their discipline. A physics student has to learn about the rules that govern the physical world. Likewise, a chemistry major must learn the basic chemical elements and how they interact. Biology students learn about plants and animals. The only discipline in which students do not learn the basic material of their discipline is education. Students take courses in curriculum, methods, educational philosophy, assessment, and classroom management. They take only one or, at most, two courses in child or educational psychology.

The basic material of education, however, is not curriculum, assessment, or methods; the basic material of education is children and youth. A teacher education program that is truly developmentally appropriate would have students major in child development. Trained in this way, a teacher would be, first and foremost, a child development specialist. Students with a strong foundation in child development can then integrate what they learn about curriculum, assessment, and management with what they know about how children think and learn at successive age levels. Without knowing about human development, the student has no central core upon which to build an integrated sense of educational practice.

From a developmental point of view, the recommendation of the Holmes Group (1989), a group of deans of schools of education from all parts of the United States, to do away with the undergraduate major in education and substitute a year or two of graduate training and internship will not produce better teachers. The Holmes Group sees the problem of teacher training as one of educational *organization,* whereas from a developmental point of view, the *content*—not the organization—of teacher training is the problem.

What needs to be far more central in undergraduate teacher training *is* not traditional education courses but study of child development. We need undergraduate departments of child development, in which students can get an integrated sequence of courses that cover the social, intellectual, and emotional development of children and youth. This course of instruction, combined with a variety of laboratory experiences that involve the student in observing and working with children, is really the only way to prepare teachers for working in classrooms.

Curriculum: An experimental approach

From a developmental point of view, several principles should guide curriculum construction.

First, a curriculum must be constructed empirically, not a priori. The way to figure out how children learn subject matter is to study how they go about learning it. It is truly a scandal that many curriculum publishers not only fail to do research on the materials they produce, they do not even field-test them. In no other profession would we allow a product to be placed on the market without extensive field testing. The felony is compounded when, after teachers have learned to cope with the problems in the curriculum, they are confronted with a new untested edition.

A truly developmental educational system would provide many opportunities for teachers to construct and test their own materials. They could see what works and what doesn't and try out different sequences and methods. The way the material works depends upon the group of children who are in the classroom that year, as well, so a curriculum should never be final but must remain open, flexible, and innovative. That sort of curriculum is exciting for the teacher as well as for the children and makes the learning and curriculum innovation a cooperative venture.

Second, and consistent with the appropriateness theme, I believe that a curriculum should be localized, particularly for elementary school children. I know that this is contrary to trends in other countries that have uniform curricula for all children. Japan and France are but two of the countries with such uniform national curricula. England, too, is initiating a uniform national curriculum in 1990. Such a national curriculum can eliminate the possibility of individualizing curricular materials to include particulars from the local environment where the children actually live and learn. Localized curricula have a great deal of intrinsic interest for children.

In learning mathematics, for example, children living in Hawaii might be asked to match coconuts and palm trees, whereas children in the Northeast might be asked to match acorns and oaks. Likewise, children's enjoyment of stories is often heightened when the stories take place in their own community or one like it. In social studies, too, children are delighted to see a picture of a building that they have actually visited. Children like stories about places and events different from their own; nonetheless, they also enjoy reading stories that directly relate to the world they live in. Children, no less than adults, appreciate both fantasy and the realism of local reference.

The idea of a localized curriculum does not, of course, preclude regional or national general curricular goals. Setting regional and national levels of achievement in different subject-matter areas is no problem as long as local schools can individualize their materials to make them more accessible and interesting to the children of that locale. The danger of a national curriculum is that it often comes to utilize uniform content for all children. It is uniform content, not the general goals of a national curriculum, that can be so deadly dull for children.

A recent Gallup poll (1989, September) indicates that about 70% of educators want national, uniform goals. If such goals are adopted, they may be translated into specific content to be taught at specific grade levels. Given the ethnic, racial, cultural, and economic diversity of U.S. society, demands for curricular uniformity directly contradict the needs for curriculum flexibility and innovation that the developmental approach prescribes.

Finally, curricula need to be studied to determine their level of developmental difficulty. Developmental difficulty is quite different from psychometric difficulty (Elkind, 1982). The psychometric difficulty of a curriculum or a test item is determined by the number of children at a particular age level who get that item correct. A curriculum or test item is usually assigned to the grade or age level at which 75% of the children at that age level pass the item.

Developmental difficulty, in contrast, must be determined by examining the "errors" that children make in attempting to master a problem or task. When young children who have been taught the short *a* sound, for example, are asked to attach the long *a* sound to the same letter, they have great difficulty. The problem is that they are being asked to grasp that one and the same letter has two different sounds. Understanding that one symbol can have two different meanings or sounds requires attainment of the mental abilities that Piaget calls *concrete operations* (Elkind, 1981). A developmental teacher would thus avoid teaching phonics until he or she was sure that most of the children had attained concrete operations.

Again, the developmental difficulty of any curriculum material cannot be determined a priori but only by active investigation. Part of the experimental work of teaching should be to explore the developmental difficulty of available curricular materials and to try new materials that might work differently or better.

Instruction: Authentic teaching

Developmentally speaking, separating the learning process from the material to be learned is as impossible as separating learning from teaching. From this point of view, the teacher is a learner as well as a teacher, and the children are teachers as well as learners. The teacher who experiments with curricula is learning about the curricula

and about the children she teaches, and children who work cooperatively with one another and who experiment with curriculum materials are teaching as well as learning.

One way to highlight the difference between authentic teaching and psychometrically oriented teaching is to look at the way question asking is handled in the two types of classroom. The teacher coming from a psychometric orientation often asks questions to determine whether or not the child has the right answer. The authentic teacher often asks questions to get information, not to test what the child knows or understands. The difference is between Piaget's semiclinical interview, aimed at eliciting the child's original and spontaneous convictions, and intelligence or achievement tests that seek to determine what the child knows or has learned.

Questioning children to discover what they think reflects the fact that the authentic teacher is first and foremost an enthusiastic learner, as well as the fact that the teacher truly believes that we have something to learn from children. We all ask rhetorical questions at times to stimulate discussion, but that type of question asking should be the exception rather than the rule.

Assessment: Documentation

Developmental assessment involves documenting the work a child has done over a given time period. Usually this is done by having a child keep a portfolio that includes some of his writing, drawing, mathematics explorations, and so on. In looking through such a portfolio, we get a good idea of the quality of work the child is capable of doing and his progress over the given time period.

Such portfolios have many fringe benefits. Not only do they inform parents of what children are doing but they provide a concrete record of a child's educational progress *for the child*. Once they are grown, many young people take great pleasure in looking over the work they have done as children. This gives them a sense of how far they have progressed and also a sense of the continuity of their development, which is nourishing to their growing sense of personal identity.

Psychometric assessment involves measuring the child's achievement by means of published or teacher-made tests. The child's progress is evaluated on the basis of her performance on the tests. In contrast to a portfolio of work, the psychometric approach provides a number or a *grade* that is intended to reflect both the quantity and quality of the work the child has done over a given time period. Numbers and grades can be a useful shorthand method for symbolizing a child's progress, but a list of grades lacks the portfolio's richness and its historical value for the young person.

Although psychometric testing is useful, it presents many risks that are currently being realized; for example, testing is often done without regard to what goes on in the classroom. Kindergarten screening tests are a case in point. Although such tests purport to measure whether or not the child is "ready" for kindergarten, they do no such thing. The tests suggest that readiness is in the child's head rather than recognizing that it exists as a relation between the child and the curriculum. How a child will do in a particular classroom depends more upon what goes on

in that classroom than upon the score the child received on a test.

We return here to the issue of transfer. The psychometric approach assumes that performance on a test automatically translates into performance in a classroom situation. By contrast, the developmental approach insists that no such transfer takes place and that to know how a child is going to perform in a classroom, you must assess that child on the challenges that he will confront in the classroom. Even at the college level, SAT scores are not good predictors of college performance. Why should we expect tests to predict better at an age when children are much more variable and much less sophisticated test takers?

Conclusion

In this essay I have tried to demonstrate that although developmentally appropriate practice as an idea is being well received rhetorically in educational circles, it faces a formidable struggle to achieve wide implementation. Without a change in underlying philosophy, changes in educational practice will be superficial at best, and this applies to the adoption of developmentally appropriate practice. No classroom or school can be genuinely developmentally appropriate when its underlying philosophy is psychometric. This psychometric philosophy explains contemporary educational inertia.

How can we get education moving in the right direction? Kuhn (1970) argues that in science, inertia is overcome when one scientific paradigm replaces another. As I indicated in the beginning of this essay, however, educational institutions are too imbedded in society to change the way science changes. Some indices of movement are visible, however, and they are coming from the means of changing social institutions that are inherent within society. One of these means is the legal system. In two states, Kentucky and Texas, the legislatures have declared the educational systems unconstitutional because the amount spent per child varies from community to community. These types of rulings will force educational reorganization.

Industry is another institution within society that may help move education in the direction of true reorganization. In some parts of the country (such as Beaverton, Oregon), each school has been adopted by a local company, which takes some responsibility for the educational program.

Finally, coalitions of educators and parents have begun to influence the state boards of education. In North Carolina such a coalition has gotten the legislature to remove testing from the first three grades. The citizens in Boston voted to have the school board appointed rather than elected in the hopes that educators will get on that ruling body.

*   *   *

Education is an enormous, and an enormously encrusted, institution, but it can move and is being moved—slowly, to be sure, but moved all the same.

References

Baron, J.B., & Sternberg, R.J. (1987). *Teaching thinking skills: Theory and practice* New York: W.H. Freeman.

Bennett, W.J. (1986). *First lessons: A report on elementary education in America.* Washington, DC: U.S. Department of Education.

Bloom, A. (1987). *The closing of the American mind.* New York: Simon & Schuster.

Bredekamp, S. (1987). *Developmentally appropriate practice in early childhood programs serving children from birth through age 8* (exp. ed.). Washington, DC: NAEYC.

Bruner, J.S., Goodnow, J.J., & Austin, G.A. (1956). *A study of thinking.* New York: Wiley.

Duncker, K. (1945). On problem solving. *Psychological Monographs, 58*(5), 1–113.

Elkind, D. (1981). Stages in the development of reading. In I. E. Sigel, D. M. Brodzinsky, & R. M. Golinkoff (Eds.), *New directions in Piagetian theory and practice* (pp. 267–279). Hillsdale, NJ: Erlbaum.

Elkind, D. (1982). Forms and traits in the conception of human intelligence. *Intelligence, 3,* 101–120.

Elkind, D. (1987). *Miseducation: Preschoolers at risk.* New York: Knopf.

Gallup Poll. (1989, September). Princeton, NJ: Author.

Hirsch, E.D., Jr. (1987). *Cultural literacy: What every American needs to know.* Boston: Houghton Mifflin.

Holmes Group. (1989). *Work in progress: The Holmes Group one year on.* East Lansing, MI: Author.

Kamii, C. (1982). *Number in preschool and kindergarten: Educational implications of Piaget's theory.* Washington, DC: NAEYC.

Kant, I. (1943). *Critique of pure reason.* New York: Wiley.

Kohler, W. (1927). *The mentality of apes.* New York: Harcourt Brace.

Kuhn, T.S. (1970). *The structure of scientific revolutions* (2nd ed.). Chicago: University of Chicago Press.

Murray, D.J. (1980). Research on human memory in the nineteenth century. In J.G. Seamon (Ed.), *Human memory.* New York: Oxford University Press.

National Commission on Excellence in Education. (1983). *A nation at risk: The imperative for educational reform.* Washington, DC: U.S. Department of Education.

Papert, S. (1980). *Mindstorms.* New York: Basic Books.

Perkins, D.N., & Salomon, G. (1988). Teaching for transfer. *Educational Leadership, 46*(1), 22–32.

Piaget, J. (1950). *The psychology of intelligence.* London: Routledge & Kegan Paul.

Piaget, J. (1952). *The child's conception of number.* London: Routledge & Kegan Paul.

Piaget, J. (1967). *The child's conception of time.* London: Routledge & Kegan Paul.

Piaget, J. (1970). *The child's conception of movement and speed.* London: Routledge & Kegan Paul.

Piaget, J. (1972). *The principles of genetic epistemology.* New York: Basic Books.

Piaget, J., & Inhelder B. (1956). *The child's conception of space.* London: Routledge & Kegan Paul.

Piaget J, Inhelder, B., & Szeminska, A. (1960). *The child's conception of geometry.* New York: Basic Books.

Ripple, R.E., & Rockcastle, V.N. (Eds.). (1964). *Piaget rediscovered: A report of the conference on cognitive studies and curriculum development.* Ithaca, NY: School of Education, Cornell University.

Thorndike, E.L. (1921). *Human learning.* New York: Century.

Weinstein, C.E., & Mayer, R.E. (1986). The teaching of learning strategies. In M.C. Wittrock (Ed.), *Handbook of research on teaching* (3rd ed.). New York: Macmillan.

Reprinted with permission from *The Care and Education of America's Young Children: Obstacles and Opportunities,* edited by Sharon L. Kagan, Ninetieth Yearbook of The National Society for the Study of Education, Part 1 (Chicago: University of Chicago Press, 1991).

3. Children's Lives Today

*A*s *I look back over the essays I have written over the years, I recognize that I was always interested in the social and historical context of child growth and development. This interest became less academic and more applied in the 1970s. Increasingly, the practices that I had assumed were limited to a few pushy nursery schools were becoming more and more widespread. Additionally, in my small clinical practice, I was seeing a large number of children who were suffering the stress of academic pressure but also of inordinate demands for self-sufficiency and maturity. Because of my concern about what was happening to children in our society, I began writing more popular articles, doing media interviews, and lecturing extensively to parents and educators as well as to professionals.*

In the late 1970s I wrote a piece for Psychology Today *on hurried children, growing up too fast too soon. The article caught the attention of Doe Coover, an editor at Addison Wesley, who asked me to write a book on the topic. I wrote a first draft that was rather dry and academic and not acceptable to Doe. She urged me to write it in a popular vein, and I did. Writing* The Hurried Child *was a very special experience. Everything I read or heard seemed to touch upon the theme. Even while reading a magazine in a waiting room, I would find examples for the book. Once I had my clippings, I wrote the book in six weeks; everything I had thought and written about for years just came together in a rush.*

The book's success showed that I had struck a chord. I agreed to write various articles about hurried children for various journals. The essay that is published here, "The Hurried Child," was written for Instructor and Teacher. *It highlights points from the book, emphasizing the hurrying that is implicit in providing early instruction in reading. The next essay, "Overwhelmed at an Early Age," is a later, more elaborated discussion of the same issue. Again I tried to relate the pressures on young children to the many changes going on in our society.*

This section concludes with a collection of questions that many parents and teachers have asked me over the years as I have tried to present my arguments for developmentally appropriate practice and for not hurrying young children. In my more than a quarter of a century of addressing parents, the questions have not changed much. Questions of early reading, full-day and half-day kindergarten, school entrance dates, and retention and transition classes are still searing questions for parents of young children. A few new questions have come up in recent years, and these have to do with multicultural education and gay parenting. In answering parents I have tried to be sensitive to their concerns and anxieties and to provide a developmental rationale for my answers.

The Hurried Child: Is Our Impatient Society Depriving Kids of Their Right To Be Children?

Pressure to succeed at all costs, pressure to cope, pressure to survive—Sound like the beginning of a list of adult stressors? It probably is, but add to it pressure to achieve before one is ready to achieve, pressure to grow up and quit acting like a child when one still *is* a child, and pressure to struggle to the top when one is only four, six, or eight years old. Combine those pressures and others, and you have the stressors we are placing on our children as we hurry them into premature adulthood.

We even want them to *look* like adults. Take, for example, the mid-teens sex symbol who sensually gyrates her hips as she models the designer jeans that are so appealing to the young. As a matter of fact, today even preschoolers wear miniature versions of adult clothing. From LaCoste shirts to scaled-down designer fashions, a whole range of adult costumes is available to children.

Three or four decades ago, boys wore short pants and knickers until they began to shave; getting a pair of long pants was a true rite of passage. Girls were not permitted to wear makeup or sheer stockings until they were in their teens. Children's clothing signaled adults that children were to be treated differently, perhaps indulgently, and children could more easily act like children; but no longer. Clothing is just one of the more obvious examples of how we hurry today's children into adulthood, pushing them toward many different types of achievement and exposing them to experiences that tax their adaptive capacity.

Look at the media, for example. Music, books, films, and television increasingly portray young people as precocious and present them in more or less explicit sexual or manipulative situations, reinforcing the pressure on children to grow up fast in their language, thinking, and behavior. Can children be hurried into growing up fast emotionally, as well? The answer is no. Feelings and emotions have their own timing and rhythm and cannot be hurried. Young teenagers may look and behave like adults, but they usually don't feel like adults. Growing up emotionally is complicated and difficult under any circumstances but may be especially so when children's behavior and appearance say "adult" while their feelings cry "child."

Academic achievement is another example of the many pressures adults place on children to grow up fast, to succeed at all costs. Society has no room for the "late bloomers," the children who come into their own later in life rather than earlier. Children have to be successful early or they are regarded as flops. This pressure to succeed has gone so far that many parents refuse to allow their children to be retained in kindergarten—despite all of the evidence that this is the best possible time to retain a child. "But," the parents say, "how can we tell our friends that our son failed kindergarten?"

A recent study of children who have been held back in kindergarten found that almost all of the parents involved were pleased with the result. They thought that repeating kindergarten had given their children, who were socially or intellectually below the norm at that time, a chance to catch up at their own speed. Many of these children were able to join their own age group later and, far from being handicapped, were helped by the opportunity to move at their own pace.

At what age should a child know how to read?

As teachers know all too well, parents hurry children when they insist that the children acquire academic skills, such as reading, at an early age (indeed, some programs now promise parents that they can teach their children to read as infants and toddlers). This pressure by parents reflects the parent's desires, not the children's needs or inclinations. Although some children gravitate to reading early, seeking out books and adults to read to them, such children seem to learn to read on their own and with little fuss or bother; but they are in the minority. Only 1 to 3 children in 100 are estimated to read proficiently (at second grade level) on entrance to kindergarten. If learning to read were as easy as learning to talk, as some people claim, many more children would learn to read on their own. The fact that they do not, despite being surrounded by print, suggests that learning to read is not a spontaneous or simple skill. The majority of children can, however, learn to read with ease if they are not hurried into it.

Children confronted with the task of learning to read before they have the requisite mental abilities may develop long-term learning difficulties. In one high school, for example, we informally compared the grades of students who had fall birthdays (September, October, November, and December) and had entered kindergarten before they were five years old with the grades of students who have spring or summer birthdays (April, May, June, and July) and had entered school after they were five years old. Boys in particular who entered kindergarten after age five rather than before had an advantage, in terms of grades.

Children should be challenged intellectually, but the challenge should be constructive, not debilitating. Forcing a child to read early, just like forcing an adolescent to take algebra when simple arithmetic is still a problem, can be a devastating experience for a young person who is not intellectually prepared for the task.

The abuse of the factory system

Schools today hurry children because administrators are pressured to produce better "products." This pressure leads administrators to treat children like empty bottles on an assembly line, getting a little fuller at each grade level. When the bottles don't get full enough, management puts pressure on the operator (the teacher, who is held accountable for filling her or his share of the bottles) and on quality control (making sure that the information is valid and the bottle is not defective). This factory approach causes schools to hurry children because it ignores individual differences in mental abilities and learning rates. The child who cannot keep up in this system, even if only temporarily, is often regarded as a defective vessel and is labeled "learning disabled" or "minimally brain damaged" or "hyperactive."

The factory mentality of our schools has been reinforced by machine-scored group testing probably more than any other single factor. Dependence on such testing has grown dramatically over the past 10 years, as parents and legislators have more vocally expressed their dissatisfaction with the schools and with children's attainments. Whether blame is placed on television, single-parent homes, working mothers, or the decline of authority, academic performance has been declining, and efforts to remedy the situation rely heavily on testing and teacher accountability. The problem with this system is that it pushes children too much, forcing them into a uniform mold. Children are being pressured to produce for the sake of teachers and administrators.

Management programs, accountability, and test scores are what schools are all about today, and children know it. Children have to produce—or else. This pressure may be good for many children, but it is bound to be bad for those who can't keep up. Their failure is more public and therefore more humiliating than ever before. Even worse, society convinces children who fail to achieve that they are letting down their parents, their peers, their teachers, the principal, the superintendent, and the school board. This is a heavy burden for many children to bear; therefore, they become much more concerned with grades than with what they know. Not surprisingly when these young people go out into the work world, they are less concerned with the job than with the pay and

the perquisites of the job. What schools have to—and parents ought to—realize is that the attitudes they inculcate in young people are carried over into the occupational world.

Schooling and education are thought of in narrow terms; the focus is on attaining basic concepts and skills. But education—true education—is coincident with life and is not limited to special skills or concepts and particularly not to test scores. Education should not come packaged or sequenced. Much of it is spontaneous, an outgrowth of openness and curiosity that must be imparted to children. Pressuring children to get certain marks on tests that, at best, measure rote knowledge is hardly the way to improve children's education. What good is education if children can read but not understand what they read or if they know how to compute but not where, when, or what to compute?

Children are hurried because we are hurried

What is the first expensive, utilitarian gift that we usually give our children? A watch! We hurry our children basically because we hurry ourselves. For all of our technological finesse and sophisticated systems, we are a people who cannot—will not—wait. We are, in short, a hurried people, and only in the context of a society that is hell-bent on doing jobs more quickly and better and is impatient with waiting and inefficiency can we understand the phenomenon of hurried children and hope to help them. First we must recognize what we cannot do. We cannot change the basic thrust of American society, for which hurrying is the accepted and valued way of life. When hurrying reflects cultural values like being punctual, then urging children to be on time has social justification. But the *abuse of hurrying* harms children—that is, when hurrying serves parental or institutional needs at the children's expense without imbuing them with redeeming social values.

Young children two to eight years old tend to perceive hurrying as a rejection, as evidence that their parents do not really care about them. Children are emotionally astute in this regard and tune in to what is a partial truth. To a certain extent, hurrying children from one caregiver to another each day, or into academic achievement, or into making decisions they are not really able to make *is* a rejection. It is a rejection of children as they see themselves, of what they are capable of coping with and doing. Children find such rejection very threatening and often develop stress symptoms as a result.

Accordingly, when parents have to hurry young children, when they have to take the children to a child care center or to a babysitter, they need to appreciate children's feelings about the matter. Giving children a rational explanation—"I have to work so we can eat and buy clothes" and so on—helps, but it isn't enough to deal with the child's implicit thought—"If they really loved me, they wouldn't go off and leave me." We need to respond to the child's feelings more than to her intellect. One might say, for instance, "I'm really going to miss you today. I wish you could be with me." The exact words are less important than the message that the

separation is painful but necessary for the parents, too.

School-age children are more independent and more self-reliant than are younger children. Consequently, school-age children often seem to welcome hurrying because they are eager to take on adult chores and responsibilities, particularly in single-parent homes, in which they may try intuitively to fill the role of the absent parent. The danger with this age group is that too often parents interpret this display of maturity as true maturity rather than what it is—a kind of game. The image to keep in mind for this age group is Peter Pan, who wanted to assume adult responsibilities but did not want to grow up and accept some of the negative qualities that children perceive as characteristic of adults. Children want to play at being grown up, but they don't want adults to take them too seriously.

We can counteract the effects of hurrying

One effective tool against the onslaught of hurrying is play. Unfortunately, the value and the meaning of play are poorly understood in our hurried society. Indeed, what happened to adults in U.S. society has now happened to children—play has been transformed into work. What was once recreational—such as sports and summer camp musical training—is now professionalized and competitive. In schools, when budgets are tight the first areas to be cut are art, music, and drama. Television and other media, suffused with the new realism, offer little in the way of truly imaginative fantasy. Perhaps the best evidence of the extent to which children are hurried is the lack of opportunities for genuine play available to them.

Children need to do more than play, of course. At every turn they are learning social rules—how to behave in a restaurant, on a plane, and at a friend's house; how to put on clothes and take them off; how to eat with utensils; how to wash behind their ears; how to dry themselves with a towel, and so on. Children can also learn basic concepts about space, time, number, color, and so on. But they need to be given an opportunity for pure play as well as for work. If adults believe that each spontaneous interest of a child is an opportunity for a lesson, they foreclose the child's opportunities for pure play.

Play is nature's way of enabling us to deal with stress, for children as well as for adults. Parents can help by investing in toys and playthings that give the greatest scope to a child's imagination—for example, a good set of blocks that give children leeway to create and that can be used for years; crayons; paints; clay; and chalk. These are all creative play materials because they allow for a child's personal expression.

Along the way, all of us—parents, teachers, and citizens—must assert the value of the arts in the schools. Overemphasizing the basics in contemporary education without a balancing emphasis on personal expression through the arts hurries children by destroying the necessary balance between work and play. The need for employees to have modes of personal expression at work is just beginning to be realized and appreciated by American industry. Schools must recognize that children also work better, learn better, and, yes, grow better if the time they spend in social adaptation—learning the basics—is alternated with healthy periods devoted to avenues for self-expression. Far from being a luxury, time and money spent on the arts enhance learning and development by reducing the stress of personal adaptation and giving children an aesthetic perspective to balance the workday perspective.

We must see childhood as a stage of life, not just the anteroom to life. Hurrying children into adulthood violates the sanctity of life by giving one period priority over another. If we value human life, we will value each period equally and give unto each stage of life what is appropriate to that stage.

We should appreciate the value of childhood with its special joys, sorrows, worries, and concerns. Valuing childhood does not mean seeing it as a happy, innocent period but rather as an important period of life to which children are entitled. They have a right to be children, to enjoy the pleasures and to suffer the trials of childhood that are infringed upon by hurrying. Childhood is the most basic human right of children.

The original version of this essay appeared in *Instructor and Teacher,* (1982), XCI(5), 41–43.

Overwhelmed at an Early Age

L
ast spring I was invited to sit in as an observer during a parent–teacher conference. As soon as the parents entered the room and sat down, I could feel the tension growing, as if the humidity were rising. The father's body language was easy to read. He sat at attention, with his arms crossed tightly across his chest and his mouth zip-lock tight. The mother was clearly distressed and kept nervously playing with the hem of her skirt. The teacher was equally uncomfortable as she tried to explain why she thought that the couple's son should repeat kindergarten. "He is a bright and pleasant boy," she told them, "but he is a little socially immature, and I am afraid he might not be able to keep up in first grade."

"You mean," the father exploded, "that my son has been in school a year and already he is an academic failure! What's wrong with you people, anyway?"

This scene, with variations, is being played out in schools across the country. One variation is the teacher telling parents who are told that their child should be placed in a transition class, which is designed to be a bit more difficult than kindergarten but not as demanding as first grade. Between 10 and 20% of kindergarten children throughout the United States are being recommended for retention or for transition classes (NASBE, 1988). Some parents are counseled—and a growing number are deciding on their own—to postpone enrolling a child in kindergarten until she or he is six years old or close to it.

For parents and educators, kindergarten has become a focus of intense interest and even greater concern. About four million children—85% of the five-year-olds in the United States—will be enrolled in public and private kindergartens in 1990, a 50% increase since 1964.

Given those numbers, the fact that early childhood education also has become an important public policy issue is not surprising. At the legislative level, there is now financial support for kindergartens in all 50 states. In addition, at least 23 states and the District of Columbia have passed, or are considering, legislation providing state funds for prekindergarten programs within public schools. Deciding which children should be admitted to these programs (and promoted within them) has produced a virulent epidemic of readiness, screening, and achievement testing of young children. Georgia was the first state to pass legislation requiring that all children be tested for kindergarten entrance and promotion. In New York City many children who enter kindergarten in September are tested at least four times before November.

Fortunately, some states are beginning to set limits on this testing fever before too many children are permanently scarred. In Mississippi, the second-to-last state to support public kindergartens, the governor removed testing from grades K–3 because it was interfering with the curriculum. Other states, such as Arizona, California, and North Carolina, are also considering or have passed legislation to limit testing of children in the early grades.

Why is kindergarten suddenly getting so much attention? The explanation lies in the interplay among three major changes that have occurred in our society over the past quarter-century. One of these has been the emergence of an "earlier is better" educational psychology, which grew out of research that began in the 1960s. A second change has been the increase, over the same period, in the number of two-parent and single-parent working families. The third change is the rapid expansion of kindergarten and prekindergarten programs in the public schools.

Is earlier necessarily better?

Since the 1960s researchers have gathered a great deal of evidence supporting the importance of education in the early years of life. Much of the initial research found that early childhood education was particularly effective for disadvantaged children. Although later studies showed that some of the early claims of academic and IQ gains from programs such as Head Start were overly optimistic, the benefits of comprehensive education and health care programs for children—together with support and job training for parents—are well established. While programs such as Head Start do not increase children's IQ, they do enable disadvantaged children to acquire the social skills and motivation to stay in school.

Understandably, many middle-class parents assumed that their children would reap comparable gains from comprehensive early childhood programs, but such programs may be less beneficial for children from middle-income families than for those from economically disadvantaged ones. An undernourished child who is put on a full-calorie, nutritionally sound diet will noticeably improve height and weight. On the other hand, an already well-nourished child placed on the same diet displays no noticeable effects. The same is true for intellectual stimulation. A child growing up in a home alive with books, music, art, and intellectual discussion will likely gain less from a comprehensive nursery school or kindergarten program than will a child growing up in a home in which television is the mainstay of intellectual stimulation.

Head Start and its impact were misinterpreted in yet another way. The name *Head Start* was an unfortunate choice because it carries the suggestion that education is a race and that an earlier start guarantees a better finish. When middle-class parents heard that children from low-income families were getting a Head Start, they naturally wanted their children to have an edge, as well, and they assumed that the way to do this was through early instruction in reading, math, and science.

In fact, the most successful programs for disadvantaged young children, including Head Start, have not been academic. The results of the Perry Preschool Study in Ypsilanti, Michigan, speak against early academic instruction (Berrueta-Clement, Schweinhart, Barnett, Epstein, & Weikart, 1984). The children who participated in the Perry Project, which offered age-appropriate learning experiences, were far less likely to be delinquent, abuse drugs, and engage in violence as adolescents than were comparably disadvantaged children who started in purely academic programs.

The educational research that has found negative effects of early academic instruction is supported by clinical observation. Dr. George M. Sterne, chair of the American Academy of Pediatrics' Early Childhood Committee, says that he and his colleagues observe two different effects of early academic pressure on young children—physical symptoms associated with stress, like abdominal pain and sleep problems, and the more specific symptoms of burnout later.

Many of these symptoms, Sterne believes, are the result of overloaded, highly structured schedules for young children, including formal teaching both in and out of school. Sterne's warnings about early academics have been echoed by our leading child psychiatrists, pediatricians, and psychologists, including Benjamin Spock, T. Berry Brazelton, and Bruno Bettelheim.

Changes in early childhood education reflect changes in the American family

Despite the consensus of research, clinical evidence, and expert opinion, the idea that young children benefit from an early start in academics, sports, or the arts is now widespread and deeply entrenched. In my opinion this popular conception has been ac-cepted largely because of the changes that have come about in the American family in recent years. In the last quarter-century, the number of women who have entered the workforce and who have children younger than age six has doubled, to more than 50%, and is expected to reach 60% by 1990. The fastest growing group of working mothers is women with children younger than age three.

Sadly, the increase in the number of affordable, high-quality child care programs has not come close to meeting the needs of these families. For many parents, locating good child care is an endless struggle and an ongoing source of frustration and anxiety.

Child care problems are not the only source of anguish for working families. Many single parents, as well as couples in which both persons work, have not entirely divested themselves of the traditional family values that prevailed when they were growing up. One of these values put a premium on one parent staying home to help the children reach their full emotional, social, and intellectual potential. When parents who still put stock in these traditional values place their preschool children in child care, they often feel guilty about not meeting their presumed parental responsibilities.

Anxious and guilty parents are ready to accept an educational psychology, however false, that will alleviate these painful emotions. When an educational psychology proclaims that young children benefit from early academic instruction—and even that they are deprived without it—then we feel comfortable enrolling children in such programs "for their own good." Many contemporary parents, often unconsciously, have readily accepted the "earlier is better" idea because it reduces their guilt. As a consequence, they have demanded academic, rather than age-appropriate, kindergarten and early childhood programs for personal rather than pedagogic reasons.

Although their feelings are easy to understand, parents should not worry or feel guilty about having their young children cared for by others. The bulk of evidence suggests that young children are not harmed but often benefit from good-quality, child-centered early education programs. In fact, such programs reduce the children's stress of separation from parents at a young age.

Public school kindergarten and prekindergarten programs have increased dramatically

The third social change that has transformed the character of early childhood education is the increase of kindergarten and prekindergarten programs in public schools. The nature of this expansion illustrates some of the problems with American education in general.

American education is in serious trouble. Modeled after American industry, it suffers from many of the ills that made American companies an easy mark for foreign competition. Education is top-heavy administratively and is overly authoritative and hierarchical. Innovation is almost totally suffocated by education's close ties to the educational publishing and testing industries. In addition, effective change is often blocked by boards of education, whose decisions may be based more on personalities and politics than upon sound pedagogy.

Until the late 1960s, kindergarten was not part of the educational establishment. Fewer than 50% of five-year-olds were enrolled. Kindergarten, moreover, was only a half-day program, and the classrooms were set up for learning preacademic concepts and skills using materials such as blocks. Children were read to rather than taught to read, and they added and subtracted beads and sticks instead of printing numbers in workbooks. They learned scientific observation by examining plants and animals, chemistry and measuring by cooking and baking, and language by talking, listening, and making up stories. The pre-60s kindergarten was well suited to the abilities and interests of young children.

All of this changed with the dramatic increase in kindergarten enrollment and with the expansion, in many communities, to full-day and prekindergarten programs. This expansion took place for the most part to meet the needs of working parents. Parents regard schools as safe havens for children. The buildings are regularly inspected, the teachers are licensed, and schools have a history of reliability and continuity that is often lacking in other child care facilities. Also, public schools are free. Given the lack of other adequate, affordable child care, parents naturally looked to the schools—which they had come to trust to care for older children—to provide for young children as well.

To the schools' credit, they did respond to this need for expanded kindergarten and prekindergarten programs. Unfortunately, however, many principals and superintendents knew little about early childhood education. They were thus unduly influenced by some parents'

demands for early academics. Moreover, when educational administrators were forced to defend their requests for funds to support these expanded programs, the presumed benefits of early academics were a strong argument. School boards, legislators, and voters are more willing to spend money for tests and workbooks than for blocks and gerbils. Many schools, like many parents, accepted and promoted the "earlier is better" educational psychology for the wrong reasons.

That is how the public school kindergarten, once flexible and independent, has become a report-card–carrying member of the educational establishment. For young children, this means that they must learn a prescribed set of skills before they can enter first grade. Rather than adapt to the educational needs of young children, schools have tried to squeeze these children onto the narrow, confined first rung of the educational ladder.

As large numbers of kindergarten children fail to make this first rung, the educational solutions are predictable: Test the child, raise the entrance age, retain the child, or put the child in a transition class. Research shows that although these solutions may work for the occasional child, they are not effective for the majority. This point was made forcibly by the National Association of Early Childhood Specialists in State Departments of Education, arguing that preschool testing, delayed entrance, and transition classes are all disguised forms of retention. Retention in any of its forms puts children at risk:

Children who have been retained demonstrate more social regression, display more behavior problems, suffer stress in connection with being retained, and more frequently leave high school without graduating [than nonretained children]. (NAECS/SDE, 1987)

Children learn best at their own pace

Clearly, there is a growing mismatch between school and young children. And it is becoming increasingly apparent that the problem lies not in young children but in those parents who demand early academics and those schools that have transformed the kindergarten into a one-size–smaller first grade. This is the real problem with "earlier is better" educational psychology. It implicitly assumes that young children are simply smaller versions of older children. It denies the enormous transformations that mark the development of intelligence between the preschool and elementary school years. Even ancient peoples recognized that children did not reach the "age of reason" until they were six or seven years old. The distance between the preschool and elementary school stages is not a step; it is a leap.

If young children are exposed to formal education before they have taken the intellectual leap that makes formal instruction meaningful, we put them at risk. Jean Piaget, the famed Swiss psychologist (1964, 1969), described one of these risks. He argued that the early years were critical for determining whether the child would become a passive learner, mastering everything by rote, or become an active learner who gains new information by discovery and invention. The early introduction of academics, before the child has the necessary mental structures to attack this learning in an inventive way, reinforces the passive mode of learning. Age-appropriate education, however, enables children to develop their active-learning modes.

Piaget's work also makes clear why the premature introduction of academics may put the child's sense of self-worth at risk. In his studies, Piaget demonstrated that children younger than six or seven think of adults as godlike creatures who are all-wise, all-knowing, and all-powerful. Fortunately, by the age of seven, children have discovered at least one thing that adults don't know. From there they proceed to the comfortable idea that adults don't know anything! But the young child firmly believes in the adult's omniscience.

Consider, then, what happens when a young child is placed in a kindergarten program and is confronted with demands to learn to read and write, requests that are beyond his ability at the moment. The child is likely to experience mental dazzle (the mental blinding produced by an overwhelming demand). Laziness or lack of motivation is not the cause; the problem is just that the child is not there yet intellectually. Formal instruction in reading and writing requires syllogistic reasoning, that is, the ability to apply a general rule to a particular case, and most young children are not yet able to do this. They cannot, for example, deduce from the rule "When two vowels go walking, the first one does the talking" that in the word "wait," the long *a* is sounded.

How does the young child deal with this situation? Unfortunately, the child does not think or say, "Hey, you dumb grown-up, I am not ready to learn these things yet; wait a couple of months, and I will gobble it up like a candy bar." What the child is likely to think and say to herself is, "These all-wise, all-knowing adults say I should be able to learn this, but I can't. I guess there must be something wrong with me; I must be dumb!" Once this idea gets stamped in, it is difficult to erase. The child interprets every success as a lucky accident and every failure as her due.

Education is not an absolute good. In America today, our schools are putting large numbers of children at risk for short-term stress and long-term learning and personality disabilities. Far too many of our children are going to school only to learn that they are "too dumb" to be there. This is not education; it is miseducation. Because our schools are creating large numbers of children with learning problems, we have a crisis in kindergarten.

How do we stop miseducating young children?

What can we do to resolve this crisis and return schools to their proper function of educating rather than miseducating children? At the policy level we have to work with schools and encourage them to institute flexible programs in the early grades. Cali-

fornia is taking the lead in this direction by working toward restructuring the entire K-through-3 curriculum to make it more developmentally appropriate. Another option is multi-age grouping, with K-to-1 or K-to-2 classrooms. By remaining in the same classroom for two or three years, each child has the opportunity to be in the oldest group, and the teacher can use what he or she has learned about the child in the first year to individualize teaching during the second and third years. Single-grade kindergartens and first grades can be made more effective if we eliminate workbooks, grades, and homework and if the classes have smaller teacher-to-child ratios. Even from a purely economic perspective, preventing learning problems is much more cost-effective than creating them and then trying to remedy them later.

Although it is clear what to do on a policy level, it is less clear what a parent should do when a child has a summer or fall birthday. The first and most important thing for parents to do is to let go of the erroneous "earlier is better" educational psychology; then they must really do their homework. A visit to the school would reveal what kind of kindergarten and first grade programs are in place. Many schools have fine kindergartens but rigid first grades. If there is a choice, parents should opt for the school with a fine kindergarten and a flexible first grade. If the program at both the kindergarten and first grade levels are regimented, parents may want to explore some alternatives. Depending on individual circumstances, holding the child out of school until the following year or putting him in a nonpressured private kindergarten or nursery school may be the best option.

Parents whose child is already in the system and who are being counseled to put their child in a transition class or to keep her back should investigate. What is the transition class and who is in it? Some transition classes are small, individualized, and beneficial. Others are large dumping grounds for children who are experiencing academic difficulty. Retention or social promotion, that is, advancing children to the next grade even when they have not reached the requisite achievement level, may be preferable to transition classes like these. Parents considering retention should ask the child how he feels about it. Some children are aware that they need more time and welcome the chance to go over the material again. Others don't like the idea at all. For children who resist, an alternative to retention and transition classes is engaging a tutor to work with the child on a one-to-one basis.

These are difficult decisions for parents to make. The couple I described at the beginning of this essay eventually accepted the suggestion to retain their son in kindergarten after first talking it over with him. He liked the kindergarten teacher and didn't mind staying with her for another year. Even so, the parents were still not entirely comfortable with the idea of their son repeating a grade. Like so many couples in their position, they had to make a "least worst" choice. The risks of retention seemed to be fewer than the risks of social promotion, but there were risks in either choice.

This couple, like so many others today who are being forced to make these decisions, are intelligent, caring, well-meaning parents. They know that the early years of schooling are critical for later academic success and want to do what is best for their children. The schools, too, want children to succeed, and schools firmly believe that delayed entrance, retention, and transition classes are effective ways to prepare children for the academic rigors of first grade.

But the crisis in kindergarten will not be alleviated by trying to make young children ready for school. It will only be resolved when schools are made ready for young children.

References

Berrueta-Clement, J., Schweinhart, L., Barnett, W., Epstein, A., & Weikart, D. (1984). *Changed lives: The effects of the Perry Preschool Program on youths through age 19.* Ypsilanti, MI: High/Scope.

National Association of Early Childhood Specialists in State Departments of Education (NAECS/SDE). (1987). *Unacceptable trends in kindergarten entry and placement.* Unpublished paper.

National Association of State Boards of Education (NASBE). (1988). *Right from the start: The report of the NASBE Task Force on Early Childhood Education.* Alexandria, VA: Author.

Piaget, J. (1964). *Judgement and reasoning in the child.* Paterson, NJ: Littlefield, Adams. (Original translation by M. Warden published 1928)

Piaget, J. (1969). *Science of education and the psychology of the child.* New York: Viking.

The original version of this essay appeared in *The Boston Globe Magazine,* September 11, 1988, pp. 18–19, 40–46, 54–58. Used with permission.

Questions Parents Ask

I n this chapter I would like to give myself a second chance. For the past several years, I have been lecturing extensively in all parts of the United States and Canada. I speak to parents, educators, and health professionals. After my lectures, if time and circumstances permit, I entertain questions. Often, long after the question-and-answer period is over, I think about my answers and wish I had answered differently or more completely. In this chapter I would like to answer again some of the questions I have been asked, but this time with the benefit of time for reflection.

Q. *You say that young children should not be taught to read and do math, but what about the child who asks you to teach her to read? My daughter kept asking me the names and sounds of the letters and how to say words she saw printed, and before I knew it, she was reading– she taught herself! Should I not have given her the names and sounds? Should I not have told what the words said?*

A. I think you did exactly the right thing. No roadblocks of any kind should be put in the way of children who want to read on their own, and we should support and encourage children in their eagerness to begin reading.

You can never miseducate children by responding appropriately to their demands for information.

But your child is the exception, for only 1 to 3% of children are reading with comprehension before they enter kindergarten. The majority of children do not show interest in the mechanics of reading until after the age of five or six, and we *do* miseducate them if we introduce such mechanics before children show any inclination in that direction.

Q. *What about discipline? In talking about trust, autonomy, industry, and the like, you don't say anything about discipline. You make it sound as if children never misbehave and that all we have to do is support and encourage. But we support and encourage our daughter, and she still defies us and gives us a hard time. What do you do when support and encouragement don't work? Can you give me some techniques I can use when she refuses to go to bed or to put away her things?*

A. Discipline is an attitude, not a technique. When we as parents feel that we are in charge of the situation, we communicate this sense of being in charge to our child. If, on the other hand, we are unsure of our ability to control our child's behavior, we will communicate that feeling as well. One of the values of knowing about child development, about how children think and feel and what psychosocial stage they are at, is that it gives us a greater sense of mastery over the situation.

But knowledge is really not enough; our own sense of competence is at issue. That is why rearing later-born children is always easier than raising first-borns. We are so much more experienced and proficient the second time around, so much more confident in our ability to handle a variety of situations, that we communicate this sense of competence to our children. It does not eliminate the need to exercise our authority, but it makes the exercise of that authority easier. In my lectures, when no one is willing to ask the first question, I say, "I will now take the second question." For many of us it would be easier if we could start with the second child!

In general, though, what is crucial to discipline is your mindset. When I see children who dominate their parents, it is always because the parents really believe that they have no control. What you need to tell yourself is that you are the adult and the child is the child. You are the one in charge and in control, not the child. And children do not want to be in charge or in control. They will take over if you let them, but it is frightening for them as well as for you. The best discipline is to say what you mean and mean what you say.

Q. *You paint a pretty grim picture of miseducation. But are we really doing such bad things to our children? OK, so we dress them up in designer clothes, send them to the gym, and have them take music lessons. So what is so terrible? What about the parents who abandon, abuse, neglect, and reject their children? We who are doing so much for our kids are the "good" guys, and what I can't understand is why you are after us and not the "bad" guys.*

A. It is *because* you are the good guys that I am troubled. When immature, self-centered, cruel people do harm to their children, it is criminal; when loving, caring, well-intentioned parents put their children at risk for no purpose, it is tragic. Of course there is nothing wrong with dressing a child in designer clothes, taking a child to the gym, or providing music lessons. But it is also a fact of life that good things misused can turn into bad things. When we provide luxuries and lessons for children at too early an age and for the wrong reasons, we endanger the child's mental health.

Q. *But do you really think that some of us parents here tonight are really doing bad things to our kids?*

A. Not really. Most of the parents who read my books and attend my lectures tend to agree with the values and child-rearing philosophy that I espouse. You read my books and come to my lectures because you want support for doing what you feel is right even though many of your neighbors and friends do not agree with you. And I try my best to give you the data and the arguments that you need to make your case. Sometimes I catch some parents who are vacillating and succeed in swinging them to the side of healthy education. But I know that the parents whom I would most like to reach will never hear me.

Q. *You seem to be against pressuring kids, but isn't pressure necessary and even good for kids? Many successful athletes had coaches who worked them hard, and many successful executives had parents who pushed them hard. I am afraid that if I don't push my child, she may just take it easy and never achieve anything in life. How do you know when to push and when not to?*

A. You have posed what is perhaps the most difficult question in childrearing. If children don't want to take music lessons, should we make them? If children don't do their homework properly, should we insist that they do it over? If children are not social, should we insist on their playing with other children? And if we do decide to pressure our children, how should we go about it? Should we offer rewards, threaten punishment, appeal to children's self-interest, or play upon their guilts and fears?

These are difficult questions, and there are no simple, easy answers to them. The only guideline I can suggest is to examine your motives. Is it really the child's welfare you are primarily concerned about, or is some personal motive or ambition the dominating factor? If you really have your child's best interests as your primary concern, then pushing a child, with whatever method is most comfortable for you, will probably do no harm. What will come through to your child is your caring enough to make the effort. Indifference is much worse.

On the other hand, if your personal motives dominate over what is in the best interests of the child, pushing will likely do harm. No one likes to be used, and when children are pressured to achieve something under the guise of doing something for themselves but really to satisfy parental need, they will eventually realize the truth. When that happens, children rebel against parental motives and methods, and the result often is just the opposite of what the parents intended.

Q. *What about television? How much should a young child watch, and what kinds of programs are "healthy" and which ones "miseducate," using your terms?*

A. A young child five years old and younger should not watch television for more than two hours a day. That is a rule of thumb, and there are exceptions, but it is a useful guideline to keep in mind. Programs like "Sesame Street," "Mr. Rogers' Neighborhood," and many of the Disney movies and programs are appropriate for young children. I don't happen to believe that the many police and detective shows are healthy for young children. The violence is even more frightening for young children than for older ones because young children may not be fully aware that the violence is only portrayed, not real. Allowing young children to watch such programs puts them at risk for fear and anxiety for no purpose because the shows have little of a positive nature to teach young children.

Q. *You seem to be opposed to lessons for young children, but my four-year-old daughter takes ballet lessons and loves them, so what is wrong with that?*

A. In general, I believe that there is no need to enroll a preschool child in a program involving formal lessons, whether it be ballet, tennis, or Japanese. I am sure that your daughter enjoys her lessons, and if she has a sensitive, knowledgeable teacher, no harm may be done. But if that is not the case, your daughter may be at risk for an injury. The bones and muscles of young children are not mature enough for strenuous exercise nor for some of the stresses and strains required by ballet, skiing, tennis, gymnastics, and so on.

As far as I am concerned, all such programs miseducate young children because absolutely no evidence reveals any long-term gain to be had from such lessons and because, at the same time, they put children at risk for physical injury for no purpose. Yes, I know that there are a number of cases of children who have started in ballet, in ice skating, or in music and have gone on to become successful professionals, but they are the exceptions, not the rule. The number of young people who were started early and who experienced failure, unhappiness, and/or physical injury is far, far greater than the number of children who started young and succeeded.

Q. *I think that you dismiss admission into a prestigious nursery school much too lightly. Many such nurseries are, after all, associated with prestigious private day schools, and children in the nursery school are likely to be given preference for admittance to the elementary and secondary schools. Having gone to the right private schools also gives a child an advantage when applying to prestigious colleges and universities. So maybe parents who are concerned about getting their children into these schools are not so silly after all.*

A. What you say is true, of course. My concern with parents' overeagerness to get their children into a prestigious nursery school is that they are doing it for the wrong reasons. If they believe that prestigious schools provide high-quality education (which they do) and that is why they are enrolling the child, there would be no problem. Too often today, however, parents enroll their children in these programs because they believe the program will start the children's academics early and thus give them an edge on the competition. Ironically, such parents, by pressuring prestigious nursery schools to go academic, are destroying the high quality of education that private schools did provide and that did give their students an edge when getting into colleges and universities.

Q. *I am divorced and have a four-year-old son, Brian. My former husband and I share joint custody. Brian is with me during the week and with his father during the weekends, some holidays, and most of the summer. I subscribe to your philosophy of not hurrying children, but my husband does not. He thinks that my son should be in an academic program, and he and his new wife are trying to teach Brian to read at home. What should I do?*

A. The only thing you can do under the circumstances is to stick to your guns. You are not going to undo what Brian's father is doing, nor are you likely to change his philosophy of education. What you must do is make very clear to Brian what he is to expect when he is with you. If he asks about reading lessons, you have to say that "there are no reading lessons in this house; if you like, I will be happy to read to you." You don't have to (and really shouldn't) put down his father or his father's education priorities. All that you need to do is assert the priorities operative in your house. That is a discrimination that a child of Brian's age can make quite well.

As to schooling, some sort of compromise would seem to be in order. A Montessori school might work. It is child centered and nonpressured on one hand but has a lot of academic content on the other. It is a program that might thus be acceptable to you both.

Q. *I am a little worried that the kind of educational programs that you are advocating for young children are old-fashioned and that what you propose is more appropriate for the 1950s than the 1980s. It is a tough world out here. Look at the extent of drug abuse, crime of all sorts, divorce, competition to get into good schools, and erosion of job opportunities—not to mention the threat of nuclear war, the proliferation of weapons, and the degradation of the environment. Is the kind of education that you propose really going to prepare children for this kind of world? Don't the people who want to start children earlier have a point? After all, there is so much to learn, so isn't earlier better?*

A. Your observation is, of course, correct: the world today is far different from what it was at mid-century. And the question you raise is really the critical one, namely, what is the best way to prepare children for an admittedly harsh and rapidly changing world? Your reaction, a natural one shared by many contemporary parents as well as by parents of the past, is to speed up the pace of education to keep up with racing social change.

The conviction that the best way to prepare children for a harsh, rapidly changing world is to introduce formal instruction at an early age is wrong. There is simply no evidence to support it, and there is considerable evidence against it. Starting children early academically has not worked in the past and is not working now; for example, in the Commonwealth of Massachusetts in the early 1800s, some 30% of two- to four-year-old children were sent to school to read and write. This action was prompted by parents and businesspeople concerned about how best to prepare children for a society that was rapidly

being transformed from an agricultural to an industrial economy. The natural impulse, then as now, was to start children earlier. Similar attempts at early schooling were started in England at about the same time by Robert Owen. Both here and abroad the experiment failed; teaching very young children to read and to write did not prove to be feasible.

In many of my writings, I have tried to marshal contemporary evidence and arguments that speak against early instruction as the best way to prepare young children for what is admittedly a harsh and difficult world. Children who go into the world with a strong sense of trust and autonomy, of initiative and belonging, and of industry and competence will be better prepared to deal with whatever the future has to offer than will children with an abundance of academic skills but a damaged sense of self. Success in life is not the product of acquired academic skills; rather, success in life is the product of a healthy personality.

Q. *I'm still not convinced. How do you know that early stimulation doesn't work? Maybe people like Glenn Doman [who has designed techniques by which, he claims, parents can start educating their infants] have something after all. Many people with innovative ideas have been put down by their colleagues, who were too short sighted or narrow minded to accept a truly innovative and important new idea. Shouldn't we give these people and their programs a chance?*

A. Certainly people with innovative ideas should be given a hearing and a chance to demonstrate the effectiveness of their programs. The problem is that most of the early-instruction programs have not been adequately and systematically researched. In the long run, as in the cases of true innovative ideas, truth will out. But truth, scientific truth, has to be demonstrated; it cannot be taken on faith. To date, the preponderance of research evidence indicates that the early "stimulation" of a child growing up in an already emotionally, intellectually, and culturally rich environment with caring parents is not going to enhance the child's brightness much beyond what it would otherwise be.

I think that we have to face the fact that there is money in miseducation, although this is not the case in healthy education. What weakens the case of the early-stimulation people is the fact that they are selling something, and it is hard to know where the truth ends and the sales pitch begins.

Q. *I know that you argue that a lot of the motivation for putting children into different programs at an early age is as much a matter of status as of genuine concern for the child. That may be good theory, but as a parent I have to face the fact that if I don't put my child in an academic preschool, he is not going to be reading when he enters kindergarten and his peers are going to be reading. Regardless of why other parents put their children in that preschool, these children are going to have a leg up on my kid if I don't put him in an academic preschool. That is a real parental, not a status, concern.*

A. I appreciate your question, even though it is a tough one to answer. In the end, it is a question that only you can resolve. I have tried to give you as much evidence as I can regarding the pros and cons of a variety of early childhood programs. I have also tried to detail the motivations that prompt parents to put children in high-pressure programs. But in the end it is up to you. If you really feel that you are doing your child a disservice by not putting him in a high-pressure program, then by all means do so. In the long run, your sense of guilt about not doing the right thing and your anxiety about whether your child will make it may have more negative effects than will putting the child in the program.

Q. *My wife and I work, and we have our three-year-old daughter, Donna, in a full-day program at a child care center near our home. The caregivers are starting to teach the children to read, and Donna now even brings home workpapers on which she is copying letters. In other respects, the place is ideal for us—convenient, clean, well run, and flexible with respect*

to hours—but we subscribe to your philosophy and would prefer that they cut out the workpapers. What can we do?

A. Talk to the director of the child care center and tell him or her about your concerns. Some centers engage in these practices because they believe that is what parents want. If enough parents protest, they will stop. If most of the parents don't feel as you do, and you want to keep your child in the facility, praise your child for the work she is doing but do not overemphasize it. Spend your time together doing things such as reading to her, playing with her, and going for excursions to interesting places. In this way you communicate your value priorities to her and put the academic experiences in proper perspective.

Q. *My son will be five years old in November, and the school entrance cutoff date is in October. I know that the school will accept him if I insist and if he has some testing, but given the "age effect" that you describe, is this the right thing to do? I also have a social conscience, and although I can afford to keep my son out for a year, I know that other parents can't, and I feel a little guilty about doing it.*

A. It is a difficult decision, and in the end you will have to follow your own conscience. Boys are particularly handicapped by being the youngest, and while this is not always the case, the probability that he will be a victim of the age effect is always there. In the end, I think that you have to do what you think is best for your child, but you can also work toward getting the school to "liberate" the kindergarten and first grade so that no child has to suffer the age effect, miseducation at its most destructive.

Q. *My child is a victim of the age effect. He also has a November birthday, but the school cutoff date was December 1, so he got in. My spouse and I were both working, and it would have been a real hardship to keep our son home or with a full-time sitter for another year. Now the school is suggesting that he repeat kindergarten because he is not ready for first grade. What should we do?*

A. Given the new data on the negative effects of retention showing that of children for whom promotion or retention has been recommended, socially promoted children do as well as children who are held back, you might want to insist that your son be promoted. If possible, however, I would also get him a tutor who could help to bring him along in his schoolwork. The individual attention provided by the tutor may also help undo some of the possible damage done by school failure to your son's sense of competence and industry.

Q. *My child is gifted and has a test IQ of more than 150. As you say, he gobbles up information. What should I do about schooling for him if, as you say, most gifted children find school boring and dull?*

A. There are several things that you can do. One is to ask that your child be promoted one grade. For gifted children the age effect does not operate, and they need the challenge of the higher grade. Research suggests that gifted children can adapt well to being the youngest and have no problem making friends, playing, and so on. Some schools have programs for gifted and talented children, and these programs can also be helpful. The only problem is that gifted children are easy to label and identify when they are singled out in this way, and that can have some negative consequences.

Anything you can do to enrich the child's experience outside the home will help, as well. There are now a number of summer programs for gifted children, who really enjoy these programs and the opportunity to be with other bright children and understanding adults. If your child has a gift in a particular area, you might introduce him to a high school or college teacher who specializes in that area. Many teachers are intrigued by a youngster who is gifted in their area and are willing to serve as mentor and to guide the child's readings and activities.

Q. *My son has been a victim of the age effect and is not doing well in school. His younger sister,*

however, has it all. She was born in the spring, while he was born in the fall. She is outgoing and lively, while he is a little shy. But most of all, she is bright and is already ahead of her brother in reading. What can we do to keep our son from feeling inferior to his sister?*

A. Accept your children on their own terms and try, as much as possible, not to make comparisons. Look for the things that your son can do well, and make sure that he is praised for them. The most important thing to do is to make your son feel loved and accepted for what he is rather than rejected for what he is not.

Q. *My daughter is in first grade, and she is already bringing homework with her from school. Should a first grade child have homework?*

A. In general, I don't approve of homework for kindergarten or first grade children. Homework is most useful as a complement to class discussion and presentations. When the teacher has the time and energy to read homework carefully, it can be a meaningful learning experience for the child. But kindergarten and first grade children still need to work on manipulatives more than on workbooks. The too-early focus on "right" and "wrong" can be a very negative experience, particularly for children who are young and struggling to keep up. There is plenty of time for homework once children have attained a healthy sense of industry and competence.

Q. *You seem to base a great deal of your argument for not introducing young children to formal instruction on the work of Jean Piaget. How solid is his work as a basis for educational decision making?*

A. Jean Piaget stands with Freud as one of the most original and productive psychologists of this century. His studies on the development of children's thinking have been repeated all over the world, with extraordinarily comparable results. His description of the stages of development thus rests upon perhaps the most solid data base in all psychology. Although Piaget did not provide curricula to be taught, his work provides powerful tools for curriculum analysis. His theory allows us, if we choose, to create curricula well suited to the child's level of mental development.

Q. *I agree with you about not pushing children, but I have a child who seems completely unmotivated. If he ever felt what you call the "structural imperative"* [intrinsic motivation derived from children's need to realize an intellectual potential or mental structure; Elkind, 1987, p. 148], *I have yet to see any evidence of it. What do you do with a child who would be happy to watch television all day long?*

A. Children do differ in the extent to which they are driven by intrinsic motivation, but all children have some of it. When children show little interest in activities other than television, they are usually using television as an escape. Their lack of motivation may stem from, for example, a fear of failure and recrimination, a fear of encountering some dangerous bits of information, or a fear of having to deal with a stressful family issue.

An unmotivated child is a stressed child. The first thing to do is to examine the child's immediate life situation. If there has been a divorce or a separation, this can trigger the fear reaction; so, too, can a move from one home and neighborhood to another, the birth of a sibling, or the death of a beloved grandparent. An overly pressured school environment can also produce the fear reaction disguised as a lack of motivation.

You can help your child recover this motivation if you can identify the major stresses in his life and do what you can to alleviate them. In the case of divorce and death, the most important thing to do is to talk with your child about these events, not just once, but many times. If the school environment is too pressured, it may be necessary to take your child out of the program and enroll him in a less pressured educational environment. What does not work and can be counterproductive is berating or teasing the child about his lack of motivation.

Q. *I am a grandmother and a "Milk-and-Cookies" mother, using your terminology. My children have all done well, thank you. My problem is my daughter-in-law. She is an incredible College-Degree parent–she has every educational program for young children known to man. There are flashcards, books, tapes, Speak and Spell–you name it, she has it. My poor grandson never has any time to play, and he is only 18 months old! Whenever he can he goes for the Kleenex box, which is his favorite toy. But his mother is always drilling him, and my son, that nitwit, lets her get away with it. What can I do?*

A. As my mother used to say, "Don't mix in." Each generation has to make its own mistakes. Nothing you can say or do is going to change what your daughter-in-law is doing. If you mix in, you will only create friction that will eventually result in your seeing your grandson less often. Use your time with your grandson to engage in the kinds of activities you used with your own children at that age. Enjoying your grandson and keeping the peace are the best things you can do for him at this point.

Q. *My situation is the reverse of that of the grandmother who spoke earlier. I have tried not to pressure my three-year-old daughter, Jean. I read a lot to her, we take walks together, she listens to records, and so on. I make sure she has time alone so she can learn to initiate her own activities. My problem is my mother-in-law. She had enrolled her daughter in Olympic skating classes when she was four years old and tried to get my husband into gymnastics. He fought it and always had to be in the shadow of his sister, and he has plenty of emotional scars as a result. Now my mother-in-law wants to get Jean started on lessons of some kind and wants to pick up the tab. What do I do?*

A. Tell your mother-in-law that you very much appreciate her offer but cannot accept it. Make it short and sweet, and don't go into details or give explanations because then you will only leave yourself open to argument. What you want to do is to give her a firm and final *no.* Go on doing what you are doing, and if the matter comes up again, handle it in the same polite but final way. Your mother-in-law will eventually get the message that this is a dead issue.

Q. *We have a home computer, and I am wondering about starting out my four-year-old son on it. What do you think?*

A. It depends a lot upon the child. You can ask your son whether he would like to play on the computer, and if he does, you might show him how pressing the keys results in something showing up on the screen. If he enjoys this, you might show him how you can write words, such as his name, and have him dictate a story to you that you can print out and read back to him. If he shows a real interest and fascination with the machine and if it has graphics capability, you might show him how to draw with the computer as an entry-level skill and eventually teach him computer games.

On the other hand, if your son does not show much interest in the machine, then I would not pursue it. You can always try again when the child is older and his pattern of interests has changed. There is really no point in insisting that a child get involved in computers when he has no inclination in that direction. By insisting when the child is not ready, you may destroy any possible interest that might develop when he is ready.

Q. *Some school systems have prekindergartens for children as young as three years old. Does the age effect operate here, as well?*

A. Prekindergartens are, in effect, a way of providing public child care for young children; they are not really kindergartens. If the programs provided are age appropriate, they can provide a useful child care serv-ice for parents. On the other hand, if they attempt to "teach" children various skills, the result could well be comparable to the impact of kindergarten—the youngest children will experience failure and all of the psychological consequences of that experience. I believe that the age effect can be observed even among three-year-olds if they are in an academically pressured environment.

Q. *How widespread is the kind of miseducation you talk about? Is it happening in other countries, as well?*

A. Canada tends to be more child centered than we are and has more age-appropriate programs. Canadian parents and educators, however, are experiencing some of the same pressures as we are here, and they may lose ground. Most of both Western and Eastern European countries do not start children on academics until they are six or seven years old, an age when most children are able to engage in symbolic and derived learning [*symbolic* in that it involves written or spoken words and numbers, *derived* in that the symbols and concepts have been created and handed down by the child's culture; Elkind, 1987, p. 140]. Nonetheless, recent cross-national comparisons of academic achievement have made countries particularly aware of their standing and have stimulated the interest of the countries involved in improving their relative standing. Unfortunately, the method often suggested, and sometimes implemented, is to start children earlier on the academic track. Although this has not happened yet, the pressures are already building in the Scandinavian countries.

Japan, of course, is special because of its extreme homogeneity of culture, tradition, and race. At the early childhood level there is more emphasis on getting children to have the right attitude, to take instruction from adults, to work hard, and to get the job done than there is on children mastering particular skills. Japanese mothers now take major responsibility for educating their young children, and this responsibility has taken its toll. Some Japanese mothers develop what has been called a "childrearing neurosis." In some extreme cases in which the mother believes that she or the child has failed, the mother may take both her own life and that of her child.

In general, the United States is about 10 years ahead of most other countries in the extent to which we are miseducating our young children. But because other countries often imitate the worst rather than the best of our social innovations, they are increasingly likely to miseducate their children, as well.

Q. *So what is going to happen? According to you, we are miseducating large numbers of young children, so what does this mean with regard to the future?*

A. I have no crystal ball and am not sure that I really want one. All that I can give you is a clinical impression, my feeling about what is to come. As I have suggested, today's parents are different from parents who reared the hurried children of the '70s and early '80s. Teenagers today are hurried children and show primarily stress symptoms, the symptoms of being pushed too hard too soon. My guess is that the teenagers of the '90s will be more neurotic than teenagers today. They will show more obsessions, more compulsions, more phobias, and more psychosomatic symptoms than do teenagers today.

What I cannot really predict is the extent of the problem. If we wake up to the dangers of miseducation at home and at school, the damage may not be too great and only a relatively small group of children will be affected. But if we refuse to recognize what miseducation is doing to our young children, we will put a significant proportion of the next generation at risk for personality problems and for occupational mediocrity.

Q. *What can we do to stop all of this miseducation?*

A. One positive thing about American society is that when we recognize a problem, we do something about it. I think that as a society we are becoming increasingly aware of the dynamics and risks of miseducation. An increasing number of professionals are speaking out against it, and the media are beginning to reflect this changed psychology. We need to reeducate all parents to the absurdity of the "superkids" psychology and to the risks of miseducation as well as to the value of healthy education. But it is not only parents who need to be reeducated; the same is true for teachers, administrators, and legislators caught up in the "competent child" mentality.

The price of liberty, it has been said, is eternal vigilance. It is also the price of healthy education. Whenever we become inattentive to the fact that children are people in their own right—with their own needs, their own special abilities, and their own learning priorities—we will likely engage in miseducation. Eternal vigilance to the special attributes of children is indeed a high price for parents and educators to pay, but the end result—healthy, happy, responsible, and productive young people—is well worth it.

*　*　*

Editor's note: All of these questions still arise frequently when David Elkind talks to parents. In recent years two new questions have been posed by many parents. Dr. Elkind takes the opportunity to address them here.

A few new questions have come up in recent years, and these have to do with multicultural education and gay parenting. In answering parents I have tried to be sensitive to their concerns and anxieties and to provide a developmental rationale for my answers.

Q. *They are teaching our kindergarten children about people of color and different ethnic backgrounds, and I am not sure that my child really grasps it all. Should they be teaching this stuff to young children?*

A. We do live in a culturally, ethnically, and racially diverse society, and our educational practice should certainly reflect that reality. At the same time, we have to be cautious, particularly with young children. It is natural for young children to think in terms of either/or, bad or good. When they are presented with information about cultural diversity, we need to make sure that the information is presented simply and that the children do not interpret difference as bad or wrong. We can do this by always empha-

sizing our commonalities: We all eat and sleep; we all get happy and sad; we all like people to be nice to us. Developmentally appropriate multicultural education helps children to appreciate our similarities as well as our differences.

Q. *Our child is in a kindergarten in which two of the children come from homes where both parents are gay. My son has shown confusion concerning the parents in these two homes. Can this be healthy for children?*

A. Children need loving, caring parents. Gay parents are as loving and caring as other parents. That said, it is certainly true that children of gay parents may well encounter a variety of negative social reactions, but these are not insurmountable. After all, children of color encounter negative reactions every day and survive quite well if they have parental love and support. Children of gay parents are not the first, nor will they be the last, children to confront social prejudice and rejection. As for your child, he will not be harmed in any way by associating with this child any more than he would be by associating with any other minority child.

Reference

Elkind, D. (1987). *Miseducation: Preschoolers at risk.* New York: Knopf.

With the exception of the last two questions and answers, added for this volume, the original version of this essay appeared in *Miseducation: Preschoolers at Risk* (pp. 184–203) by David Elkind, 1987.

Afterword

You have now had a chance to review some of my reflections on early childhood education. I hope that I have conveyed how much I have enjoyed, and how much I have learned from, working with young children and their teachers over the years. Many times, as I was saddened and embittered by what I was seeing happening to young children in all walks of life, I would talk to teachers or visit classrooms and get rejuvenated. Despite the many forces working against the well-being of children today, the courage and commitment of parents and teachers make me cautiously optimistic about the future. I do believe that we are moving, however slowly, toward vital families and vital schools that will celebrate human life, human learning, and human development.

Information About NAEYC

NAEYC is . . .

. . . a membership-supported organization of people committed to fostering the growth and development of children from birth through age eight. Membership is open to all who share a desire to serve and act on behalf of the needs and rights of young children.

NAEYC provides . . .

. . . educational services and resources to adults who work with and for children, including

• *Young Children, the* journal for early childhood educators

• **Books, posters, brochures,** and **videos** to expand your knowledge and commitment to young children, with topics including infants, curriculum, research, discipline, teacher education, and parent involvement

• An **Annual Conference** that brings people from all over the country to share their expertise and advocate on behalf of children and families

• **Week of the Young Child** celebrations sponsored by NAEYC Affiliate Groups across the nation to call public attention to the needs and rights of children and families

• **Insurance plans** for individuals and programs

• **Public affairs** information for knowledgeable advocacy efforts at all levels of government and through the media

• The **National Academy of Early Childhood Programs,** a voluntary accreditation system for high-quality programs for children

• The **National Institute for Early Childhood Professional Development,** providing resources and services to improve professional preparation and development of early childhood educators

• The **Information Service,** a centralized source of information sharing, distribution, and collaboration

For free information about membership, publications, or other NAEYC services . . .

. . . call NAEYC at 202–232–8777 or 800–424–2460, or write to . . . NAEYC, 1509 16th Street, N.W., Washington, DC 20036–1426.